CO-AQX-858

The First R:

Fundamentals
of
Initial
Reading Instruction

by R. Baird Shuman

A National Education Association Publication

Note

The opinions expressed in this publication should not be construed as representing the policy or position of the National Education Association. Materials published as part of the Developments in Classroom Instruction Series are intended to be discussion documents for teachers who are concerned with specialized interests of the profession.

Library of Congress Cataloging-in-Publication Data

Shuman, R. Baird (Robert Baird), 1929–
  The first R.

  (Developments in classroom instruction)
  Bibliography: p.
  1. Reading (Elementary)—United States.   I. Title
II. Series
LB1050.S467   1987   372.4'1   86-21798
ISBN 0-8106-1833-8

CONTENTS

The Author

R. Baird Shuman is Professor of English and Director of English Education at the University of Illinois at Urbana-Champaign. He is also the author of *Strategies in Teaching Reading: Secondary*, and the coauthor of *The Beginning Teacher: A Practical Guide to Problem Solving*, published by NEA.

The Advisory Panel

Cynthia R. Coley, first grade teacher, Gillett Elementary School, Wisconsin

Gary Manning, Professor of Education, University of Alabama at Birmingham

Maryann Murphy Manning, Professor of Education, University of Alabama at Birmingham

Evelyn R. Miller, Curriculum Resource teacher, Orange County Public Schools, Orlando, Florida

Lynette F. Moody, Reading teacher, New Hope School, Wilson, North Carolina

Pamela R. Smith, teacher, Quarter Mile Lane School, Bridgeton, New Jersey

Marla M. Streit, Media Center Director, Bourbonnais Upper Grade Center, Illinois

Chapter 1
A LOOK AT READING INSTRUCTION

WHAT IS READING?

Reading is a term that people frequently use, and yet no two people define it in quite the same way. No single, universal definition of reading, accurate and usable at all times and in all situations, has yet been advanced. If asked what reading is, the average person would probably say something like "You know, it's with a book, like when you read it." Such a definition, circular and inexact, is really a nondefinition. More sophisticated people, those who have given some thought to the matter, would arrive at a more exact definition, but they would, nevertheless, find the term difficult to define in any comprehensive way—and many of them would disagree about each other's definitions. Those who have considered how broadly reading can be defined might note that we *read* people's facial expressions or that an airline pilot might respond to a controller who has just communicated with him or her verbally, "Yes, I *read* you." We all know that reading has occurred when people give sound to symbols—words or notes of music, for example—and produce utterances:

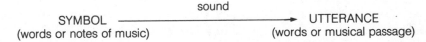

This is a limited form of reading, however. Someone might achieve this level of reading by producing the sounds, "John went away for two reasons: he was bored with his job and he didn't want to marry Myrtle." If, after reading this sentence, the reader is asked, "Why did John go away?" and she or he answers, "I don't know," some people would say that the reader has not read the passage. Others would say that indeed the reader has *read* the passage but has not comprehended it.

If you do not know German, which is a quite phonetic language, you can give utterance to—by some definitions, you can *read*—"Ich liebe dich," even though you may not know what it means. Hence, while giving utterance to symbols is reading, it is reading narrowly defined. Such reading can be useful in some situations. If you call home and are told by your young sister that you have received a postcard from Germany written in German, you might say, "Read it to me." If your sister is able to read "Ich liebe dich" and the name signed beneath this revealing statement, even though she does not understand the message, she has conveyed it to you.

In hearing and understanding the message, you use your sister's limited reading ability in German to bring you to the next level of reading ability—that of comprehension. But in this situation, you probably would not be identified as the reader; your sister would be. On the other hand, if you yourself read the postcard's message, "Ice liebe dich," and know that someone is saying "I love you," you are reading at a level one step beyond that achieved by your sister.

$$SYMBOL \xrightarrow{\text{sound}} UTTERANCE \xrightarrow{\text{thought}} MEANING$$

In this diagram, sound and thought may be virtually simultaneous, in which case utterance and meaning may also coincide:

$$Symbol \xrightarrow{\overset{\text{sound}}{}\underset{\text{thought}}{}} \begin{matrix} UTTERANCE \\ MEANING \end{matrix}$$

IS READING DECODING OR COMPREHENSION?

The great debate that Jeanne Chall writes about in *Learning to Read: The Great Debate* (1)* is partially a debate between those who stress phonics in reading, thereby enabling students to read "Ich liebe dich" without necessarily knowing what it means, and those who stress comprehension to the extent of saying that merely to utter the words "Ich liebe dich" after having seen them on a page is not a legitimate form of reading.

To those who have thought little about it—and especially to those who have long been able to read easily with good comprehension—the debate may seem inconsequential and silly. However, the way teachers lean in this debate will very much affect the way they approach the teaching of reading to primary school students who cannot read. The debate, therefore, is one of considerable importance and moment.

It is doubtful that anyone who supports the phonics approach to early reading instruction would deny the importance of comprehension in

---

*Numbers in parentheses appearing in the text refer to the Notes beginning on page 141.

reading. Such people differ from those who stress comprehension in early reading instruction only in regard to the question of when comprehension should be stressed.

Perhaps at this point you are thinking, "What good does it do to read if you don't know what you've read?" It seems obvious that reading is a tool the essential function of which is to unlock from symbols the meanings embodied in them. However, Nila Banton Smith approaches the question historically in *Why Do the Schools Teach Reading as They Do?* She writes: "For centuries absolutely no attention was given to teaching children how to get the thought from what they read. If they had learned to 'pronounce the words' their reading achievement was supposed to have been completed. . . . No attempt was made to teach pupils to read for meanings nor to check their reading after it was done to find out how much of the content they had absorbed" (2).

On the other hand, Neil Postman writes, "The modern idea of testing a reader's 'comprehension,' as distinct from something else a reader may be doing, would have seemed an absurdity in 1790 or 1830 or 1860." He asks: "What else was reading but comprehending? As far as we know, there did not exist such a thing as a 'reading problem,' except, of course, for those who could not attend school. To attend school meant to learn to read, for without that capacity, one could not participate in the culture's conversations" (3).

Obviously, Smith and Postman are talking about two different populations and two different levels of reading. Smith focuses on initial reading instruction; Postman focuses rather on the reading for ideas that more mature readers engage in.

The modern tendency is to differentiate between mere decoding and reading with comprehension. Bruno Bettelheim and Karen Zelan are particularly concerned about this matter. They cite Benjamin Bloom's research as suggesting that "approximately 50 percent of general achievement at grade 12 (age 18) has been reached by the end of grade 3 (age 9)," (4) thereby pointing out the importance of the early instruction students receive. They urge that when children are learning to read, great emphasis be placed on making students want to be literate. They feel that interesting students in content (which requires comprehension) is fundamental if students are to develop a positive inner attitude toward reading that will stay with them throughout their lives. They go so far as to suggest that decoding be taught separately from reading for ideas (5).

Bettelheim and Zelan also caution primary school teachers not to use only books with pictures in them because students at this stage may become too dependent on pictures for clues to the meaning of what they are reading. They say, "Being able to guess from the pictures what the accompanying text is all about, a child who initially is uninterested in reading sees no reason to struggle with learning the words when he can get ample information from the illustrations" (6).

Wilma H. Miller identifies stages of reading development in children and places comprehension after the development of such skills as sight word recognition, phonic analysis, structural (morphemic) analysis, picture clues, and contextual analysis (7). She does not say precisely how these stages fit into the learning sequence in primary classrooms, but she implies that a number of them can be taught simultaneously. She does not suggest anything so drastic as teaching decoding divorced from comprehension as Bettelheim and Zelan do.

WHAT PRIMARY SCHOOLS STRESS

The debate about how to teach reading is more heated among primary school teachers than among most other people. This is because primary school teachers are continually confronted with the problem of how to teach reading to a diverse group of first, second, and third graders, all of whom have different backgrounds that will drastically affect their ability to cope with the printed word.

If primary school teachers can get their students to sound out letters and to combine these sounds into words, they may understandably think they have helped their students to learn how to read. Few would disagree that students who have gained the ability to sound out words have taken an important initial step in learning how to read. Some reading specialists argue, however, that reading accomplished in this way, devoid as it may be of comprehension, does students little good and, indeed, may help to establish bad reading habits that will later make it difficult for them to become fast and effective readers.

A crucial question at this point is whether children should be encouraged to fix their eyes on individual letters (C–A–T or M–A–N, for example) or on word configurations (CAT or MAN) or on still larger units such as phrases or clauses. Much more will be said about this matter in a later chapter.

This question and a number of others related to it have engaged the attention of teachers of reading for years; they have also caused many notable linguists to explore the whole question of how people learn to read and of how they can best be taught to read. Researchers have also recently become quite concerned with the physiology of reading, with learning more about the capabilities of the eye muscles of young readers (8).

READING INSTRUCTION AND THE MODERN LINGUISTS

Leonard Bloomfield's *Language* (9), published in 1933, was instrumental in defining modern linguistics. Bloomfield demanded that the study of language be more scientific and objective than it had previously been and demonstrated how such an end could be accomplished. He was concerned essentially with the spoken rather than the written language, and he insisted that grammar be based upon the forms and structures found in language as it is actually used, not as some purist thought it should be used. He considered that any language at any time represents a complete system of sounds and forms existing independently of the past. Such thinking, in its day revolutionary, led the way to a whole new conception of language study and linguistic understanding. Moreover, Chapter 28 of *Language*, "Applications and Outlooks," provided a linguistic framework for many scholars and teachers who sought to use linguistics to devise more effective means of teaching reading.

In 1942, Bloomfield published his much-cited essay "Linguistics and Reading" (10). As early as 1937, however, he had given considerable attention to the teaching of reading, largely because he was concerned with how his own young son was being taught to read. Bloomfield told the noted lexicographer Clarence L. Barnhart that he had devised a system of reading instruction for his own son "because the methods used in the schools were nonscientific in nature and ignored the fundamental principles of scientific study of language developed during the last 150 years" (11). Barnhart contends: "Bloomfield's system of teaching reading is a linguistic system. Essentially, a linguistic system of teaching reading separates the problem of the study of word-form from the study of word-meaning" (12). More will be said later about Bloomfield's approach to reading instruction. It is sufficient at this point to note that in the initial stages, it focused essentially on acquainting students with the *phonemes* or elemental sounds of the language and on teaching them how to combine these phonemes into meaningful utterances (*man, pat, pin*, for example) as well as utterances that have no meaning (*mip, nim, pos*, for example) but that are, nevertheless, pronounceable.

Bloomfield postulated that "in order to read alphabetic writing one must have an ingrained habit of producing the phonemes of one's language when one sees the written marks which conventionally represent these phonemes. . . . The accomplished reader of English, then, has an overpracticed and ingrained habit of uttering one phoneme of the English language when he sees the letter *p*, another phoneme when he sees the letter *i*, another when he sees the letter *n*" (13).

Charles C. Fries, writing almost two decades after Bloomfield, asserts that "One can 'read' insofar as he can respond to the language signals represented by patterns of graphic shapes as fully as he has learned to respond to the same language signals of his code represented by patterns of auditory shapes" (14). He warns that "contrary to the belief of many, *written material contains less of the language signals than does talk*" (15). Fries is concerned with having readers respond to units larger than phonemes, and he considers reading to have occurred only when comprehension has occurred: "Real reading is *productive reading*—an active responding to all the sets of signals represented in the graphic patterns as they build up, *and the carrying forward of such a complete cumulative comprehension as makes it possible to fill in the intonation sequences, the special stresses, and the grouping pauses that the written text requires to fill out its full range of signals*" (16). Clearly, he does not consider the expressionless sounding of words to constitute reading in any real sense.

Fries gleaned complexities in reading instruction that eluded Bloomfield. He addresses one of these complexities in the introduction to *Linguistics and Reading*: "One can learn such words as MAN, MAT, MEN, MET, the phonics way and project similar letter-sound correspondences through a substantial number of words. But even for the three letter words like MAN it is not the single letter *A* that indicates the vowel sound. . . . It is the spelling-pattern *MAN* in contrast with the spelling-patterns *MANE* and *MEAN* that signals the different vowel phonemes that identify these three different word-patterns /maen/ /men/ /min/; or MAT /maet/-MATE /met/-MEAT /mit/" (17).

Fries makes quite sophisticated differentiations, and comprehension is obviously an underlying ingredient in all of them. So it is in much of the work of most of the notable psycholinguistically oriented writers in the field—Frank Smith, Kenneth Goodman, Yetta Goodman, and Paul Kolers. Another member of this group, George A. Miller, reminds his readers that "The pen in 'fountain pen' and the pen in 'play pen' are very different pens, even though they are phonologically and orthographically identical. The words in a sentence interact" (18). Comprehension is indisputably a necessary component of the interaction to which Miller alludes.

CURRENT CONCERNS IN TEACHING READING

Reading teachers have long been concerned with matters related to word attack, vocabulary building, word study (prefixes, suffixes, derivational roots, etc.), study skills, reading in specialized or content areas, oral reading efficiency, pronunciation, spelling, and the speed and accuracy with which students read. These concerns persist, but with the advent and growth of linguistic science, new light has been shed on the understanding of many of them.

As teachers of reading came to understand more about human psychology, particularly about the psychology of young children, the question of reading readiness became, and has remained, a prominent concern. Of all the reading researchers who warn against pushing children into reading experiences too early, perhaps none have stronger objections to using such materials as basal readers at the kindergarten level than do Miles A. Tinker and Constance M. McCullough. They remind kindergarten teachers that research indicates "that a half year or year later [after kindergarten] a child can learn the same things faster" (19).

Largely through the research of socio- and psycholinguists, attention has lately been focused on two extremely important areas of reading instruction, *miscue analysis* and *dialectology*, as they relate to reading achievement. Kenneth Goodman and Yetta Goodman are the pioneering investigators in the area of miscue analysis. Later researchers in language—Kenneth R. Johnson, Roger Shuy, Ralph Fasold, Joan Baratz, William Stewart, William Labov, and Jane Torrey—have focused attention on the relationship of dialects to reading ability.

Certainly, a new era in the understanding of language began with the publication in 1957 of Noam Chomsky's *Syntactic Structures*. This book marked the rise of transformational-generative grammar, a system with which some reading researchers had, in one way or another, been dealing earlier. A year before the publication of Chomsky's book, William S. Gray wrote about sentence analysis and transforming, using the model sentence "The water in our village well is good to drink" and analyzing it as follows:

> As one reads the first two words in this sentence various associations are aroused. This grasp of meanings is restricted and made more definite as the third, fourth, fifth, and sixth words are recognized. The thoughts then retained are held in mind, as the reader continues to the end of the sentence. When he recognizes the words, "good to drink," the meaning already acquired is greatly expanded and clarified. The final idea is the result of the fusion of the meanings of the separate words into a coherent whole. (20)

11

Gray goes on to note that the simple shifting of the verb "is" to the beginning of the sentence leads to the interrogative transformation. Early attuned to much of the linguistic questioning and investigation going on in the 1950s, Gray was quick to see the implications of linguistic science, and particularly of the transformational-generative approach to language study, for reading instruction.

TEACHING TO THE BICAMERAL BRAIN

Despite the great advances made in learning theory in recent years, we have obtained relatively little detailed information about the physiology of how people learn. Promising recent research has sought to explain more fully the workings of the whole brain, including the right hemisphere. It is the right hemisphere that has to do with intuition and non-linear thinking. No wholly conclusive results are yet available, nor are they likely to be in the foreseeable future, although researchers have taken promising tentative steps in this area. It is certainly apparent that only a small portion of the brain's full potential has been tapped and that modern schools teach to the left rather than to the right hemisphere.

The National Society for the Study of Education devoted one of its two 1978 Yearbooks to an investigation of how the brain operates and of what this portends for the educative process. *Education and the Brain* (21) is an important book. Also of considerable interest in this area are Robert E. Ornstein's *The Psychology of Consciousness* (22) and *The Nature of Human Consciousness* (23), Jerome S. Bruner's *The Process of Education* (24), Robert Samples and Robert Wohlford's *Opening* (25), Robert Persig's *Zen and the Art of Motorcycle Maintenance* (26), and Robert Sample's *The Metaphoric Mind* (27). Denny T. Wolfe's chapter "Reading and the Brain" in *English Teaching and the Brain* (28) deals directly and succinctly with the question of the teaching of reading and the bicameral brain. Although Wolfe has more to say about the teaching of reading at the secondary level than at the elementary level, the chapter has significance for elementary school teachers.

Certainly much well-accepted modern theory suggests that reflection has a great deal to do with learning and that the mind, once it absorbs a bit of information, no matter how inconsequential that bit of information may seem, retains it at a subconscious or unconscious level, even though perhaps not at a conscious one. As we learn more about how to activate the mind's amazing retentive powers and to bring required information into the conscious sphere when it is needed, teaching and learning techniques will change drastically.

The right brain deals holistically with data. In most people, it is the intuitive, metaphoric region of the brain. It tends toward making analogies, toward dealing with whole gestalts or shapes. This differentiation appears to have a great deal to do with initial reading instruction when young children are dealing with the shapes and forms of letters and of words.

The left hemisphere, which is the verbal center in most people's brains, is certainly much engaged in the early stages of reading instruction, but teachers often ignore the potential of the right hemisphere in their eagerness to get young students to read and write. Actually, most children are largely right-brained when they first come to school, but once there, the emphasis on activities that engage the left brain—and they are emphasized because they yield measurable outcomes—often crowds out activities that engage both hemispheres. By offering such activities, teachers could perhaps ultimately lead children to more significant learnings and understandings than are available to them if all teaching is essentially aimed at the rational rather than the metaphoric, at the objective rather than the subjective, at analysis rather than synthesis.

Chapter 2
PATHWAYS TO READING

Reading, as was noted in the preceding chapter, involves both the physical act of decoding and the more cerebral act of comprehending, of knowing what words say and mean. Some readers who can decode do so in complete isolation. They read words, but not sentences—printed symbols, but not ideas or concepts. Although decoding is a necessary concomitant of reading, it must be viewed as a means rather than an end. The ultimate responsibility of reading teachers is to help their students to develop the ability to comprehend what they are reading. Probably the best way to do this is to provide youngsters with situations and activities in which they realize that reading is an effective means of finding out about things they want to understand better.

ARE GOOD READERS BORN OR MADE?

The kinds of environments in which children spend their first five years will have much to do with their attitude toward and their ability in reading. When Jeanne Chall was asked what could get youngsters off to a good start in reading, she answered unhesitatingly: "Reading to children at home helps. Reading to them in nursery school and kindergarten helps." She suggests: "Read them stories, first of all—interesting stories that are vital to children. From the stories, then I would have them learn some of the key words—some easier, some harder. I would have a program of phonics, or decoding, which builds gradually and which relates to the stories they are reading" (1). Chall acknowledges that youngsters who come from homes in which reading is valued and is frequently engaged in have a distinct advantage over students who come from homes in which reading is not commonly practiced. However, she believes initial disadvantages in reading can be overcome if teachers of young children involve their students in transactions with literature as early as possible.

Paired reading at home—that is, reading in which children read aloud something they enjoy while a tutor (a parent, in this case) reads along with them, giving a perfect example of mispronounced words and making sure that the reader pronounces each word correctly—is particularly valuable for young children. This procedure leads children to independent reading: "When the child feels confident enough to read a section of text unsupported, the child signals by a knock, nudge, or other gesture for the tutor to be silent" (2). Paired reading can take place in the school setting by having older students serve as tutors for beginning readers on a regular basis. The program works best if the reading does not last too long but does occur with regularity.

Research by Jerry L. Johns supports Chall's suggestion that children whose parents read to them will have an advantage when they begin to learn how to read. Johns's study reveals that when the Sands *Concept About Print Test* was given to 60 first grade students, equally divided among below-average, average, and above-average readers, "above-average readers were superior to below-average readers in print-direction concepts, letter-word concepts, and advanced-print concepts" (3). Success in each of these concept areas is attributable in one way or another to a child's being read to and having thereby gained a familiarity with books and with print.

Reinforcement in the home of what is being learned in school will be of great advantage to any student. Chall not only suggests that parents read to their children who have not yet learned to read but also urges that parents continue to show an interest in their children's reading by helping them to read more difficult books as they progress in school. Chall thinks the books many teachers use are too easy for students who have shown growth in their reading abilities, and she encourages teachers to direct students to books slightly above their reading levels.

Certainly many of the books to which young readers have been exposed are not enticing to today's students, who have been brought up on television and who expect that their reading fare will be at least as well-constructed and exciting as *Sesame Street*. Bruno Bettelheim and Karen Zelan remind teachers that if they use books that are vacuous, empty of ideas, all they can stress is decoding, and that their young, impressionable students may well come to think that decoding is the most important aspect of reading (4). As noted previously, these researchers go so far as to suggest that phonics and other mechanics of reading, the learning of which requires drill and repetition, be separated initially from the reading process so that children will associate reading with ideas rather than with purely mechanical processes.

If the aim of reading instruction is to get students to comprehend what they are reading, teachers should expose them to stories on a regular basis. Students in nursery school and kindergarten should be read to and should be encouraged to compose their own stories. Teachers should write these stories on sheets of paper, printing them in block letters, displaying the teller's name prominently on them, and posting them where people can see them. These stories should be brief, not extending beyond one page of large print. If the print is colorful, as it will be when it is done with crayons or colored markers, it should attract attention and should make the students whose compositions are posted feel good, not only about themselves but also about stories, about writing, and about reading.

IDENTIFYING EARLY READERS

Recent research by Gary Manning and Maryann M. Manning classifies the characteristics of early readers from low socioeconomic backgrounds. In home interviews with the parents of such children, as well as the parents of children who were not early readers, they found that the early readers "(1) prefer quiet games; (2) prefer to play with older children; (3) enjoy playing alone; (4) attended structured preschools; (5) prefer educational TV programs to cartoons; (6) watch TV fewer hours a week; (7) check out books from the library with their parents; (8) have parents who read for pleasure; (9) have parents who believe they should help them with reading; and (10) have parents with slightly more years of schooling than parents of nonreaders" (5).

Significant in this report is that the parents of early readers tended to be readers themselves. Although they had spent only slightly more years in school (13.6 years for mothers and 13.8 years for fathers) than the parents of the nonreaders (12.1 years for mothers and 11.5 years for fathers), they had, on average, some postsecondary education, which is a crucial matter.

THE ART OF QUESTIONING

Even in an age of great competition from television, teachers can make stories dramatic and interesting. The story is a superb vehicle for stimulating student imagination, and teachers can enhance student response to stories by asking specific types of questions about what has been or is being read. Teachers should be guided in framing their questions about stories by what is currently known about the kinds of information various questions solicit.

P. David Pearson and Rand J. Spiro have identified three types of questions, each of which occupies a different position in the hierarchy of learning. Their classification includes the following types of interrogation:

1. Questions that require text-explicit information (How many sisters did Cinderella have?)
2. Questions that require text-implicit information (What do you think Cinderella's stepmother wants for her own daughters?)
3. Questions that require script/schema-implicit information (How did Cinderella feel about her stepmother?) (6)

The first type of question tests whether students listening to the story have retained the simple factual details it presents. The second type is more interpretive, although information specifically given in the story provides the answer to it. The third type of question is much more interpretive and speculative. To answer it, students must read implications into the story and must arrive at an answer by drawing information from their own knowledge, which not all students are in a position to do.

Questions can, as Karen K. Wixson concludes, "lead readers away from as well as toward desirable learning outcomes" (7). Wixson reminds teachers that "questions must be considered within the context of both the reader and the text, rather than in isolation" (8) and that they must take into account the reader's existing knowledge. In other words, given a heterogeneous group of students, teachers should ask all three types of questions, thereby making it possible for students at various levels of development and from diverse backgrounds to have an opportunity to respond. Teachers must be cautioned not to reach premature judgments about student ability on the basis of who answers which types of questions and of how valid their answers are. Preschool children and children in the primary grades develop at quite different rates, and one who is presently performing at the purely literal end of the spectrum may experience a growth in insight that will change that situation quite quickly.

WORDS IN THE CHILD'S ENVIRONMENT

Children who are exposed to an urban environment are continually bombarded by words on signs and in other contexts that are a natural part of such an environment. Many two- and three-year-olds can identify McDonald's, Wendy's, Burger King, the Holiday Inn, or the Ramada Inn because not only have they learned to make associations that may be related in part to word recognition but also they can recognize the designs that surround the letters.

Yetta Goodman and Bess Altwerger feel that the logos with which we are surrounded are important devices that can help very young children come to their first recognition of the fact that print has meaning (9). From this standpoint, the logo can be a useful teaching device in the preschool, kindergarten, and first grade. Recognition of logos can be encouraging to young students, and one cannot deny that such recognition bears a close kinship to reading at a rudimentary level.

It is possible to use logos in making up printed stories which will help students become familiar with the concept of the book. In one experiment, Shelley B. Wepner created such books from dictation by two groups of children, one group about 3.5 years old and the other group 4.5 years old. Students pasted logos in their books, and each book was individually tailored to each student. She kept the vocabulary simple and familiar, and used such sentences as "Jessica loves Burger King." She had students read their books to each other and to her; as they did so, she tape-recorded their readings so that they could later hear themselves reading.

Wepner found that this technique was successful up to a point, and that it familiarized students with many of the elements of a book and of print. The 4.5-year-old students also began to recognize the beginnings and ends of stories so that they were starting to internalize some of the structural characteristic of writing (10). Wepner's techniques worked well for the students with whom she was working.

Other research questions whether young students who recognize logos are actually reading. Working with four-year-old Australian students, Marilyn Goodall found that many of them could identify such words as *McDonald's*, *Band-Aid*, and *Coca Cola* when they were shown these terms in isolation (11). The Wepner and Goodall studies certainly point to the fact that logos can be used successfully as devices for teaching very young students to read only if they are in some way associated with other print and with familiar words.

Certainly the four-year-old student who can begin to gain a concept of what a book is and of what print is and what the relationship is between the two will have a headstart in reading. If, as Wepner suggests, some of these students also come to recognize some of the structural elements in story lines, they will have gained a sophistication that will be useful to them as they move into the primary grades.

UNDERSTANDING STUDENT ERRORS

Work in miscue analysis, which is addressed in Chapter 9, has led teachers to realize that they can learn a great deal about their students if they understand the kinds of errors students make in decoding. With students who are just learning to read, some types of errors may indicate sophistication rather than deficiency.

Bettelheim and Zelan tell of a bright kindergarten student who was frequently read to and who was just beginning to read on her own. In this instance, she was reading a story about a monkey on stilts, the last sentence of which was "What fun!" The word *fun* had occurred previously in the story, and the child had read it correctly. When she came to the end of the story, however, she read, "What fail!" and had a puzzled look on her face.

An initial surface reaction in a situation like this might be for the teacher to conclude that the student does not really know the word *fun* and that she has read it correctly in its earlier occurrences because the context gave her clues. But just the opposite may also be the case. In this instance, the student was not enjoying the story. Her previous encounters with stories had led her to believe that the conclusion of a story sums up the story. Because she had not enjoyed the story, "What fun!" was not an accurate summary statement, and her substitution of "What fail!" represented her conclusion about the story (12).

This child had achieved a degree of literary sophistication that enabled her to make generalizations about story structure—in this case, about the function of final statements in stories. Therefore, her misreading, if interpreted on a deep rather than a surface level, might well lead a teacher to conclude that the child is advanced for her age. Research on correlations between students' understanding of story structure and comprehension suggests that "some young readers are aware of text structure and this awareness is correlated with recall of important textual information" (13). Studies by Gordon Bower and by Jean Mandler and Nancy Johnson clearly indicate that if students have an awareness of story structure, they will remember the stories better and will become more proficient at predicting the outcomes of stories (14), a skill that reflects a high level of reading sophistication.

Lesley Mandel Morrow contends that an awareness of story structure will also help students to differentiate "between major and minor events, see relationships between events, and know what to expect in a story" (15). Although Morrow's research focuses on students who are already able to read, it also has significance for children who are on the brink of being able to read. If they have, through being read to, begun to glean elements of story structure, as had the child in Bettelheim and Zelan's example, they are on the path to becoming efficient and sophisticated readers.

ORAL LITERATURE AND STORY STRUCTURE

Oral literature has through the ages been an important vehicle for transmitting culture. Societies concerned with trying to achieve universal literacy date back only a century or two in most cases. Before the populace could read and write, most of the history and folkways of civilizations were transmitted through the oral recitation of tales such as *Beowulf*, *Gilgamesh*, and *The Song of Roland*, and of the fairy tales of the Brothers Grimm. Nursery rhymes are a fundamental part of our oral tradition and occur in one form or another throughout all cultures.

Oral literature, much of which is now available on records or tapes, can provide prereading students with an excellent bridge to reading; such literature is intricately structured and a great deal of it is at an interest level appropriate to young children. Stories such as "Little Red Riding Hood," "Hansel and Gretel," "Cinderella," and "Jack in the Beanstalk" are solidly placed in the oral tradition of the United States as well as many other countries.

Oral tales are useful because they incorporate the structural devices that will help students learn how to read them in their printed form after they have been exposed to them orally. Because the tellers of tales had to remember what they were to present them to audiences who were familiar with their stories—and most of the *gleemen* of old who wandered around reciting their tales had committed thousands of lines to memory—the tales contained specific memory aids that can be used effectively in early reading instruction.

Carol Lauritzen has identified the four most common of these aids: (1) repetition of wording; (2) repetition of syntactic patterns; (3) the use of linking words; and (4) cumulative structure (16). Lauritzen suggests that students be introduced to the oral version of a story or poem, and that they be moved gradually toward printed versions of the material.

When printed versions are read from, much of the initial reading will be retelling more than reading, but, as Lauritzen suggests, "the constancy of an oral literary pattern provides a great deal of security for beginning readers and remedial readers" (17). She also notes that students who begin their reading in this way do not seem to engage in the "hesitant, jerky, word-by-word reading" that often characterizes the oral reading of young children. This statement suggests that the students are doing more than merely decoding. They know the story, which is designed to bear repetition, and their reading of it involves a level of comprehension that usually is lacking when they read from some of their other books.

REREADING FAVORITE BOOKS

Some teachers feel that rereading a book that a class has already read once is a waste of time. Among young children, however, repetition is often valuable. Just as children learn language by constantly repeating phrases—often to the point that their repetitions drive adults to distraction—so they can learn something about story structure by the repeated reading of books that they particularly like.

Miriam Martinez and Nancy Roser worked with two groups of four-year-old students, one group in the home and the other in nursery school. They classified student responses to stories according to form (did the student ask a question, answer a question, or make a comment) and focus (whether what the student said was directed toward the story's title, characters, events, details, setting, language, or theme).

The study revealed that children in both the home and the school settings talked more as they gained familiarity with the story. Their talk also changed in form as the story became more familiar. As the story was repeated, the children's responses focused on different aspects of the story than they had at first. As students grew more familiar with the story, the depth of their understanding increased substantially, indicating that the rereading of stories is far from a waste of time but is rather a step toward the development of greater skills in comprehending what the story is about (18).

It is necessary to remember that young children are in the process of discovering their own worlds and that to impose an adult concept of time upon them is perhaps to rob them of some of the joys and rewards of discovery as well as to reduce the level at which they are comprehending the materials to which their teachers are leading them.

UNDERSTANDING WHERE YOUR STUDENTS COME FROM

Teachers who do not know much about the cultures from which their students come may experience difficulty in teaching these students. Students from some cultures, for example, will not look teachers in the eye because they have been taught that it is disrespectful to look directly at people in positions of authority. Navajo children have been brought up to value the spirit of cooperation over the spirit of competition so they may find themselves at a loss in a situation that is essentially competitive.

Developing sensitivity to the backgrounds and cultures of students can help teachers to work most effectively with those students who come from cultures different from their own. A teacher's lack of understanding of such cultural differences can lead to devastating results for young children and, in some cases, can turn them off to learning forever.

The Kamehameha Educational Research Institute in Hawaii has devoted itself for many years to the development of instructional programs and strategies aimed at increasing the achievement of Hawaiian children. The program recently served students in 65 classrooms in five different public schools on the islands of Oahu, Hawaii, and Kauai. The program stresses that reading instruction shall be meaning oriented.

The Institute has identified three areas in which students working in culturally compatible situations will learn best. To begin with, the classroom has an open-door policy; students are permitted to enter the classroom as soon as they arrive at school. The second policy, that of having several learning centers in the classroom, is derived from an acknowledgment that Hawaiian children are given many responsibilities at home. In school, they are given the responsibility of setting up the learning centers that will be used during the day, providing them with the sense of involvement they feel at home but might be deprived of in conventional school settings. Thirdly, reading discussion is carried on in such a way that individual children are not called on. Rather the group talks about whatever it is they are focusing on and the group provides answers to questions.

Many a child who was considered below average has blossomed in the experimental programs of the Institute; the explanation for this improvement—the Institute has recognized the culture of the learners and has adapted its instructional policies to harmonize with that culture (19).

Probably no greater barrier exists to effective instruction than that posed by the clash of cultures. In a society as diverse as that found in the

United States and in many other industrial nations, it is imperative that those teaching the young know as much as they can about the cultures from which their students are drawn. Failure to understand these cultures will result in failure to understand the students who come from them. Students who find themselves in schools where their own cultures are not understood or valued will soon sink to the lowest end of the education spectrum and will ultimately fail in school and possibly in life.

Chapter 3
HOW YOUNG CHILDREN LEARN

Imitation rather than scientific design accounts for the teaching styles of most educators. We teach as we were taught because it seems safe to teach this way. We survived it so we presume that our students will survive it and perhaps prosper as we did. Communities will accept without question the endless grammar drill, the recitation of multiplication tables, and other exercises such as these that have characterized the educations of the people in the power structure of any advanced society. Methodology is questioned only when it departs significantly from what was done when those who control education were in school.

Had medicine been subjected to the public pressures that have normally been exerted on education, in all likelihood we would still be treating people by bleeding them, and the average person would not live to be 50. Schools change slowly, and even when valid and compelling research evidence is available to educators, that evidence is often held suspect and is slow to make inroads in many schools.

CLASSIFICATION OF EARLY LEARNING PROCESSES

Numerous classifications can be made of the learning processes of young children. A strict chronological classification, while extremely generalized in nature and rife with exceptions, can be of some help to parents and teachers. Frances L. Ilg has arrived at a useful taxonomy. After tracing the events in children's development that lead to reading readiness (1), she associates each of these events with a typical age at which it might be expected to occur. For example, between two and two and a half years of age, children are generally interested in tiny things, including "a tiny edition of Kate Greenaway or Peter Rabbit" (2). This positive feeling about one or more books, even though it may have little or nothing to do with the physical act of reading as such, is a first step toward the acceptance of books. Between the ages of two and three, children may develop a sustained interest in the stories parents tell or read to them; between the ages of three and three and a half, they may memorize stories or nursery rhymes. When one reads familiar favorite stories to children of the latter age group, it is interesting to change one key word

24

(for example, to substitute "bird" for "butterfly") to see whether the child notices the substitution and suggests the correction.

Ilg comments that the young child who is frequently read to begins to build up a store of sight words, often based on the word's initial letter and on the memory of a story. She speculates that between five and a half and six, the child "can read the word *Washington* as easily as *Jane* if the story is about Washington and he can recognize this word because it begins with *W*..." (3). Among other useful generalizations that Ilg makes are the following:

- The typical first grader approaches reading with zest and enthusiasm, but will likely have trouble keeping his or her place because of the instability of the visual mechanism at that age.
- Youngsters at six may insert words, especially adjectives, into what they are reading aloud, particularly adjectives they have just read because at that age they love repetition.
- Such youngsters begin with enthusiasm, but their interest may flag because they cannot sustain it for long.
- They become mechanical readers as they approach age seven, reading in a virtual monotone, presumably because they are now becoming increasingly concerned with comprehension which may be decreased if they stop to labor over every word (4).

Ilg's findings, based upon extensive observation of large numbers of children, were little influenced by the findings of neurophysiologists, much of whose most important work became available after Ilg had enunciated her conclusions about child development. The same might be said of many of the findings of Jean Piaget, who also made important generalizations about the way children develop intellectually and physically.

RECENT NEUROPHYSIOLOGICAL FINDINGS

Recent research in neurophysiology suggests conclusions of enormous significance to educators. In many instances, the neurophysical findings support the earlier speculations and empirical findings of such seminal thinkers as Piaget, Vygotsky, Chomsky, and—much earlier—Montessori, Whitehead, and even Aristotle. Montessori was a physician; her approach to learning and teaching methodologies was often based upon strong biological evidence as well as upon philosophical and pedagogical speculation.

Herman T. Epstein has recently chronicled the brain's physical growth, noting that "human brain growth occurs primarily during the age intervals of three to ten months and from two to four, six to eight, ten to twelve or thirteen, and fourteen to sixteen or seventeen years, and . . . these stages correlate well in timing with stages in mental growth" (5). Epstein notes that all stages of growth in the brain—except for the last stage, 14 to 16 or 17—correspond almost exactly to the classical stages of development identified by Piaget.

If Epstein's research is valid, as it appears to be, then teachers should take careful note; it indicates that periods exist when intellectual effort will yield more significant results than an equivalent amount of intellectual effort might yield at some other time. Also, as will be seen, to begin intellectual training prematurely may produce long-term negative results so that the early starter may ultimately become the student who falls behind. Students who are pushed into tasks prematurely may fail at them and may, as a result, begin to develop images of themselves as failures.

Epstein's (and Piaget's) third stage is crucial. It is during this stage that initial reading instruction is emphasized and most children learn to read. Although some notable experts in the field have suggested that reading instruction should begin before the first grade—as noted in Chapter 4, which deals with reading readiness—Epstein's findings discourage early reading instruction. Two notable studies have revealed that learning is best achieved if students are not pushed into reading before they are ready.

R. S. Hampleman did a longitudinal study of two groups of children, the first consisting of students who were no older than six years and three months when they entered school and the second consisting of students who were six years and four months of age or older when they entered school. The overall intelligence of each group was essentially the same. By the end of sixth grade, the group of students who had entered school at a later age (the older group) was approximately one-third of a year advanced over the younger group. The difference, while not statistically significant, is certainly suggestive (6).

Of greater statistical significance are the findings of L. B. Carter who compared two groups of 50 children each: the first group entered school before age six; the second entered school after becoming six. The two groups were intellectually similar, and the balance of boys and girls was controlled. The Carter study reveals that by the end of sixth grade, a full 87 percent of the children who entered school prior to age six had not equalled the scholastic achievement of the group whose members en-

26

tered school after becoming six (7). These findings are important when viewed in the light of Epstein's findings about the physiological stages in the brain's development.

Although some researchers have found it possible to teach reading to first grade students who have a mental age of less than six years, their evidence speaks merely of teaching students to do something—in this case, to read—but fails to take into account the long-term benefits of doing so, as the Hampleman and Carter studies have done. Albert J. Harris acknowledges that it is possible to teach children of mental ages below six to read; but in seeking to do so, he warns, one must expect that progress will be slower, the teacher effort greater, and the need for individualization considerably more than when teachers work with children whose mental development is further along (8).

As early as 1923, E. L. Thorndike, concerned with the question of readiness in relation to the physiology of the brain, discussed the behavior of neurones and their possible effects on intellectual achievement at various developmental stages (9). Arnold Gesell was also concerned with the question of humankind's stages of physiological development and their implications for education (10). Their conclusions suggesting that human development is a highly individual matter certainly lead one to be cautious about trying to teach students to read before they are ready. More success will be experienced if children are enticed by ideas and if they move into reading when their natural curiosity leads them into it.

OPPOSING VIEWS

The next chapter notes that some highly respected researchers in reading call for earlier beginnings in reading instruction for some children. Notable among the authorities cited is Dolores Durkin who has long had an interest in and a concern with this matter (11). Durkin does not advocate pushing children prematurely into reading, but she feels that some children have the desire to read early and that reading instruction would not be harmful to them. Their desire is easily noticeable. They are children who love to be read to, who develop a good store of sight words, and who have an interest in printed signs and other printed objects. These children generally come from environments in which books are important. They are generally middle- or upper-class children. But even these children, it must be remembered, may not in all cases possess the visual stability to be able to read well in any sustained way (12), so there is no cause to worry if they are not amenable to early reading instruction.

The frantic abandonment and disparagement of progressive education in the period immediately following the launching of Sputnik in 1957 caused many influential educators to push toward developing learning strategies that would enable students to learn things earlier. Influential among the books of the time was Jerome S. Bruner's *The Process of Education*, which startled readers with such statements as, "We begin with the hypothesis that any subject can be taught effectively in some intellectually honest form to any child at any stage of development" (13). One must remember that this statement was presented as a hypothesis to be tested rather than, as many took it to be, a statement of Bruner's theory of education. But, because this fact was not fully realized, some educators thought that the ages of children and the stages of their development had less to do with their learning processes (including learning how to read) than the organization of the material taught to them did.

Perhaps the most interesting and carefully considered approach to early reading instruction comes from Lawrence Kohlberg, who, while not denying the mental growth that occurs between ages six and eight, feels that reading instruction might reasonably be undertaken earlier. He writes:

> A good deal of learning to read and to write in the elementary school is a tedious task for the six to eight year old, requiring drill, repetition, self-correction and considerable insecurity in comparing the child's own performance with that of other children in the classroom. Because reading and writing (especially reading) are relatively low level sensorimotor skills, there is nothing in the cognitive structure of the reading task which involves any high challenge to the older child. In contrast, the identification of letters and words can be challenging fun for younger children. (14)

One must acknowledge the validity of Kohlberg's statement *for some children*. However, the physical development of the individual child, as well as the environmental factors that impinge on his or her learning readiness, will inevitably dictate that some children cannot begin to read early and will not profit from doing so. Indeed, by attempting to read before they are ready, their first formal learning experience may become a frustrating one, and it is sometimes difficult for children who associate frustration with the first formal learning tasks to disassociate frustration from them in the future. Therefore, if teachers (and/or parents) are going to err in this particular matter, less harm is likely if they err by keeping the child longer than necessary from formal instruction rather than by pushing the unready child into premature learning situations.

THE MIND AS RECEPTOR

The human brain is never at rest; it is always actively involved in a variety of processes. Even when children are engaged in such seemingly passive activities as listening to someone talk, viewing television, or being read to, complex and active mental processes are occurring in them. Teachers can help to control and shape experience, but each individual must process that experience, and each will process it in a different way. Neurophysiologists have found substantial evidence "that environmental stimulation helps the 'healthy' brain develop to its optimal condition" (15). Teachers can help to provide some of the environmental stimulation alluded to here. They have less control over how students process what they receive than they have over making sure that students receive some stimulation.

Consistent with recent discoveries about the brain and its workings, Robert M. Gagné writes that many changes have taken place in the conception of how people learn and of what learning is. He notes: "investigators are shifting from what may be called a *connectionist* view of learning to an *information processing* view. From an older view which held that learning is a matter of establishing *connections* between stimuli and responses," he continues, "we are moving rapidly to acceptance of a view that stimuli are processed in quite a number of different ways by the human central nervous system, and that understanding learning is a matter of figuring out how these various processes operate." Gagné acknowledges, "Connecting one neural event with another may still be that most basic component of these processes, but their varied nature makes connection itself too simple a model for learning and remembering" (16). This statement is, of course, provocative in view of much that has been written by Bruner (17), Bloom (18), and other learning theorists.

Whether learning to read is regarded as a passive or an active learning experience—and cases have been made for both views—it can never be said convincingly that the mind is not involved actively in the learning process. David H. Russell claims: "The act of reading has usually been regarded as a receptive process rather than a creative one. There seems to be some justification, however, for the use of the term 'creative reading' to signify behavior which goes beyond word identification or understanding of literal meaning to the reader's interpretation of the printed materials" (19). In this statement Russell strives to relate reading to his six major categories of thinking behavior—perceptual thinking, associative thinking, concept formation, problem solving, critical thinking, and creative thinking. What he says, however, is quite in agreement with the conclusions of other researchers about the kind of process involved in learning to read—particularly the conclusions of those researchers who think that reading has not occurred if comprehension has not taken place.

Piaget was aware that "it has been shown by the study of animal behavior as well as by the study of the electrical activity of the nervous system that the organism is never passive, but presents spontaneous and global activities whose form is rhythmic" (20). Teachers must remember that they are dealing always with sentient beings who mold the experiences that reach them into their own interpretations of those experiences. The mind as receptor is never passive. It receives, it perceives, it retrieves, it translates, it transforms, it assimilates, and, in the end, it retains its own image of all that has been imprinted upon it.

INCREMENTAL LEARNING

Most teaching is based upon the fact that learning is incremental. Good teaching is a partnership between teachers and learners because it is well-acknowledged that the more responsibility learners assume for their learning, the more effective the learning experience is. Bloom's taxonomy and Bruner's theory of instruction are based on the incremental nature of learning. Both stress that learning must be accomplished in small, sequential steps, with the behavioral outcome of each step clearly and specifically stated in advance. For example, in beginning reading, an outcome (behavioral objective) such as "The student will learn the Roman alphabet" would be much too broad. Rather, a reasonable objective might be "The student will learn to distinguish between the lowercase block letters *b* and *d* in a printed context." Behavioral outcomes are never stated in such terms as "The student will learn to appreciate . . ." or "The student will come to understand . . ." because appreciation and understanding are not measurable in specific ways. On the other hand, a teacher can show students a picture of a boy and a picture of a dog and ask which one begins with /b/. The answer given will be either correct or incorrect, and will be a valid test of the stated objective.

Madeline Hunter, who defines learning as "any change of behavior that is not maturational or due to a temporary condition of the organism," goes on to say, "Learning is governed by laws and proceeds incrementally" (21). Few would quarrel either with Hunter's definition, which she supports very well, or with her statement about the incremental nature of learning; however, her latter statement cannot be taken at face value without considering some other theories about the incremental nature of learning, of which more will be said subsequently.

Hunter supports her second statement by saying, "Learning is incremental. Simpler learning components make up more complex learning behaviors. Therefore, we can systematically build step by step toward a complex learning. The acquisition of a more complex behavior attests to the accomplishment of the necessary component or prerequisite learnings" (22). Hunter calls for precision in the teaching process and suggests that "attainability by the learner within a reasonable time is another essential property of an appropriate learning objective" (23). Each of Hunter's statements contends that all learning is incremental. Nowhere does she state that it continuously proceeds from one increment to the next *at the same rate*. Anyone reading such an implication into Hunter's statements—and such misreadings have not been uncommon—may possess a distorted view of what she is calling for. It may well be in many cases that although increment B comes logically after increment A, some students are not ready to move from one level to the succeeding level at a particular time. Fallow periods in a child's development occur at particular times between one level and the next. Such fallow periods occur in the learning sequences of all human beings; in some cases they last for a year or more and can be followed by spurts in learning potential, *if the fallow periods are handled properly*.

THE CRITERION OF DIFFICULTY

Albert North Whitehead, writing in 1922, made statements that fly in the face of much that later learning theorists, such as those just mentioned, came to espouse. Nevertheless, Whitehead's arguments are so cogent that no one who is concerned with the question of how people learn can ignore them. Indeed, neuroscientists are now beginning to present research evidence to support many of Whitehead's earlier contentions.

Whitehead first states that "different subjects and modes of study should be undertaken by pupils at fitting times when they have reached the proper stage of mental development" (24). Such a statement is so patently and universally acceptable that one might ask why Whitehead would take the trouble to make it. Indeed, taken at face value, this statement seems to be completely consistent with what Hunter and

Bloom and Bruner have contended. However, when Whitehead takes the statement one step further, its content takes an unexpected turn; he urges his reader to "consider first the concept of difficulty. It is not true that the easier subjects should precede the harder. On the contrary, some of the hardest must come first because nature so dictates, and because they are essential to life" (25). He goes on to speak of the enormously difficult challenge that language acquisition, one of the most complex and confusing learning tasks known to the human race, presents to society's youngest learners. He continues, "The hardest task in mathematics is the study of the elements of algebra, and yet this stage must precede the comparative simplicity of the differential calculus" (26).

WHITEHEAD'S THEORY OF NECESSARY ANTECEDENTS

Whitehead is more concerned with the question of necessary antecedents in the learning process than he is with moving from simple to less simple to complex, as Hunter delineates the process and as Bloom and Bruner both suggest. Whitehead says that a student *cannot* read *Hamlet* if a student cannot read. In terms of difficulty, learning to read presents learners with much greater challenges than does reading a specific work after they have learned to read. But the initial skill must be learned, regardless of difficulty, before the second act can be accomplished. Many learning theorists appear to ignore or forget this basic and quite obvious fact. In so doing, they may cause teachers to underestimate the degree of challenge that some early elements of reading instruction present to their students (27).

It may be difficult, for example, for a teacher to understand why some students can identify the word *boy* or *toy* or *girl* on one page of a primer and then, five minutes later, be unable to identify the same word on another page. Teachers who are puzzled by this phenomenon should look at a page of Arabic or Chinese or Hebrew or Greek and find one symbol on the page. Then they should scan the page looking for a repetition of the symbol. It is devilishly difficult to spot such a symbol when one is unused to the language and symbol system being used, and this is just the sort of problem with which beginning readers are faced.

ADJUSTING THE PACE OF LEARNING

Whitehead addresses the question of whether intellectual progress is continuous or, as he calls it, periodic. This argument is the basis for his title, "The Rhythm of Education." He writes, "The pupil's progress is often conceived as a uniform steady advance undifferentiated by change or type or alteration in pace; for example, a boy may be conceived as starting Latin at ten years of age and by a uniform progression steadily developing into a classical scholar at the age of eighteen or twenty" (28). Whitehead uses the word *rhythm* to convey the sense of "difference within a framework of repetition." He is convinced that learning activity, like life, is periodic.

Although Whitehead is less explicit than Piaget about the ages at which various stages of development occur, there is remarkable correspondence between what the two writers think. Whitehead believes that the three years between the ages of 12 and 15 represent the optimal time for a massive attack on language; he suggests, following this period, that a massive attack on science is appropriate. This contention is consistent with the stages of romance, precision, and generalization that he identifies.

Research in the physiology of the brain indicates that no new brain cells are formed after the second year of life; however, "the cessation [of the production of brain cells] contrasts markedly with the increase of about 35 percent in brain weight after [age two]" (29). Epstein argues: "If these modifications occur continuously during child development, then each child at any age represents a point on a continuum of development. However," he cautions, "if increases are not continuous, but rather occur at discrete periods during life, then we have to think in terms of *stages* of brain development. Such brain development stages may well manifest themselves in correlated, if not causally related, stages of mental development" (30).

Epstein's data indicate that the theory that the brain's weight increases in stages rather than continuously is provable, and that these stages occur between 2 and 4 years, 6 and 8, 10 and 12, and 14 and 16, with some variations attributable to gender differences (31). These stages of the brain's physical growth are well correlated, as Epstein says, with stages of mental development. Epstein suggests that "the question of what to do during the putative 'fallow' period will be answered definitively only by executing in schools (not in psychology laboratories!) some well-designed experiments aimed directly at that question" (32). The answer to that question can have a great deal to do with the whole of anyone's intellectual development. Perhaps, as Kohlberg suggests, the "relatively low level sensorimotor skills" (33) such as reading (decoding) and writing would best be taught during the fallow periods so that the more intellectually interesting tasks, such as comprehension, can be approached when the mind is in a growth stage. But it is equally possible that the complexities, both physical and intellectual, of initial reading and writing experiences are best handled when the brain is in a growth phase. The data on this matter are sketchy and inconclusive to date.

THE BICAMERAL BRAIN

As early as Aristotle's time, the brain was recognized as being bicameral. In most people, the left hemisphere governs the actions of the right side of the body and vice versa. It is now thought that in most people, the left brain controls such operations as reasoning, analyzing, speech formation, linear thinking, verbal activity, sequential patterning, and comparing and contrasting. The right brain, on the other hand, is concerned with intuition, synthesis, the holistic view of things, subjectivity, and analogical processes. The left brain is alert, the right brain aware; the left brain is controlled, the right brain creative; the left brain is knowing, the right brain absorbing; the left brain is active, the right brain receptive (34).

We know little about the intricacies of how the brain processes information. We do know, however, that some experiments show ways in which an increased knowledge of the functions of both hemispheres of the brain can drastically change the way in which initial reading instruction is offered. Roger Sperry experimented with patients, mostly stroke victims, whose corpus callosum had been severed, causing their right and left brains to function independently of each other. Sperry flashed on a screen for one-tenth of a second words like KEYCASE, in such a way that KEY appeared only in the left field of vision, CASE in the right. When he asked patients what word they had seen, they said CASE. But when he had them reach into a bag and pull out the item that corresponded to the word they had seen, they consistently pulled out keys—even though they could not name what they had pulled out (35).

In a study of a Japanese patient whose left middle cerebral artery was occluded, Yamadori reports that the patient could read Japanese ideograms (Kanji) but had great difficulty reading Japanese phonograms (Kana), presumably because reading the phonograms depended on the left hemisphere while reading the ideograms depended on the right (36). Extensive research has determined that "pictures, generated images, and instructions to image words" (37) can have a profound effect on the retention of information presented to both adults and children.

Reporting on one of his own experiments, Merlin C. Wittrock writes: "In reading, learners are hypothesized to use individualized abstract analytical and specific contextual cognitive processes to generate meaning for the text from their memories of earlier experiences. The sentences in the text are the retrieval clues which initiate the generative processes. In one study of reading," Wittrock reports, "one familiar synonym substituted in each sentence for an unfamiliar word doubled children's comprehension of the story and sizably raised their retention of it" (38). Such information is becoming available in such volume that it will in all likelihood have a profound effect on the strategies of future reading instruction as well as on the way that future beginning reading materials are composed.

Chapter 4
WHEN ARE CHILDREN READY TO READ?

READINESS DEFINED

Among the many definitions of reading readiness, there is perhaps none more succinct and direct than Ethelouise Carpenter's serviceable statement that "readiness lies somewhere between wanting to and having to" (1). Alexander and others call reading readiness "the systematic teaching of skills used to translate print into a comprehensible message" (2). In essence, children are ready to read when they show signs of realizing that written words have meaning, that words are composed of letters that have sounds, and that words can be combined into phrases, clauses, and sentences to produce fuller meanings.

Readiness is a process of becoming, a process of bringing together the vast complex abilities and, in some cases, materials required to perform a task, be it walking, talking, reading, digging a hole, baking a cake, or whitewashing a fence in Hannibal, Missouri. Underlying readiness is curiosity, and this is where motivation comes in. Without curiosity, no one is ever ready to embark on a learning experience. Although the physical development of the eye muscles and other such factors enter into reading readiness (3), youngsters cannot really be said to be ready for reading until they need to know something that the printed medium can tell them.

The factors that determine reading readiness are so numerous that it is impossible to recognize all of them. They are different for every child. David P. Ausubel warns that "readiness can never be specified apart from relevant environmental conditions" (4). Albert J. Harris goes beyond this statement, contending that readiness is influenced significantly by intellectual development, language development, perceptual development, sociocultural factors, and personality development (5).

Ausubel agrees essentially with Harris when later in his study he states, "Readiness is a cumulative developmental product reflecting the influence of all prior genic effects, all prior incidental experience, and all prior learning (i.e., specific practice) on cognitive patterning and the growth of cognitive capacities, as well as the interactions among these different variables" (6). Ausubel calls readiness "the principal developmental dimension of cognitive structure" (7).

Cunningham and others acknowledge most of the conventional components of reading readiness, but they also stress the importance of communicating to children some of the salient purposes of reading as well as helping them gain familiarity with terms they will need to know in relation to reading (8). The metalinguistic terms that apply to reading—*letter*, *word*, and *sentence*, for example—sometimes seem so obvious that it does not occur to teachers to teach them. However, without a knowledge of the basic vocabulary of reading, students have difficulty learning to read (9).

In her examination of the teacher's manuals accompanying five basal reading series, Dolores Durkin discovered that not all of them paid attention to the metalanguage students have to know in order to be able to talk about language and to understand it. She writes: "If a manual suggested that a period be describd to students as something that shows where a sentence ends, that was considered comprehension instruction. Although it was lean, the directive was judged to be both relevant and instructive, since readers do need to know where sentences end if they are to understand them." Durkin goes on to say, "Before being told about this function of periods, however, they [students] need to know what a sentence is, but manual authors overlooked this need" (10).

Certainly teachers should also expose students to happy situations that involve reading and should demand that their basal readers and other materials used in initial reading instruction depict people reading for pleasure and for information (11). Few basal reading selections show people actully reading.

Edward W. Dolch lists five kinds of readiness that he considers necessary before a child can embark most productively on the task of reading: physical readiness, school readiness, language readiness, interest readiness, and perceptual readiness (12). Dolch may be correct in assuming that readiness in all these areas is prerequisite to learning to read effectively, but in pointing out the areas in which children need to be ready, he suggests obliquely the sorts of real problems that today's teachers have in dealing with the diversity of students found in typical primary grade classrooms.

THE CURRENCY OF THE TERM *READING READINESS*

Although the term *reading readiness* came into common use in the 1920s, "the common interpretation was that readiness is the product of maturation" (13). Durkin shows how the psychology of G. Stanley Hall has directly influenced the conception of readiness in reading instruction, based as it was on the belief that "each individual, as he grows and develops, passes through certain stages, and these stages follow each other in an inevitable, predetermined order" (14). This mechanistic view of human development has a certain neatness and an appealing order about it; vestiges of it are found even today in Kohlberg's stages of moral development and in similar taxonomies. But this view does not suggest that one should merely wait for learning to happen rather than directing activities toward well-defined learning ends.

Ausubel recognizes that "to equate the principles of readiness and maturation not only muddies the conceptual waters, but also makes it difficult for the school to appreciate that insufficient readiness may reflect inadequate prior learning on the part of the pupils because of inappropriate or inefficient instructional methods." He then warns of a prevalent danger: "Lack of maturation can then become a conveniently available scapegoat whenever children manifest insufficient readiness to learn," thereby absolving the school of responsibility (15).

Miles A. Tinker and Constance M. McCullough, while not denying the importance of maturation in reading readiness, believe that a child "is ready to read when maturation, experience plus verbal facility and adjustment are sufficient to insure that he can learn in the classroom situation." They classify the factors involved in reading readiness as follows: "(1) intelligence and socio-economic status; (2) physical factors; (3) experience and language development; and (4) personal and social adjustment" (16).

Some writers suggest that one cannot afford to wait for maturation to occur in beginning readers. Michael A. Wallach and Lise Wallach warn: "Waiting for readiness to mature is hard to justify ... if there is something one can do to facilitate acquisition of the skill in question. The social consequences of waiting are to hold down those who are disadvantaged already" (17). The Wallachs agree with Durkin, who suggests that disadvantaged children need, "instead of a postponement in reading instruction, ... an early start with it" (18). To dismiss such children with the excuse of waiting for them to mature is to deprive some of them of instruction in an area that can help them to become integrated more fully into the mainstream of their society.

Nevertheless, not all children are ready to read at the same time. Research by George W. McConkie and David Zola suggests that some children do not have the physical coordination of the eye muscles that effective reading demands; they are physically unable to read efficiently until this coordination develops (19). Attempts to teach them to read prematurely may have a pernicious effect on their later ability to read. When they fail or are inefficient in their early attempts to read, they may form an image of themselves as deficient readers. Such a stigma can interfere significantly with their attempts to read after their eye muscles have developed to the point that they are physically able to undertake the task. Also, reading will not be a pleasurable experience for children who have to struggle too hard to perform the skill, and such children are unlikely to grow into enthusiastic readers. Teachers should deal with these children by reading to them, by letting them know that interesting stories and exciting information are contained in books, so that their motivation for learning to read will be enhanced every day they are in school.

The first book on reading readiness was M. Lucile Harrison's *Reading Readiness* (20), followed three years later by *Methods of Determining Reading Readiness* (21). For the last six decades, readiness has received considerable attention from teachers of reading and from researchers in the field. Questions remain about how readiness is best determined and about what instruments are most reliable for measuring it. However, it is generally thought that students should be enticed into reading rather than forced into it before they are physically and psychologically ready to undertake the task of learning the single skill that will likely have the most significant long-term effects on all of their formal learning experiences.

WHEN ARE CHILDREN READY TO READ?

No pat answer to the question "When is a child ready?" has proved satisfactory. In fact, in the light of recent research, such answers seem dangerous. The simplest and most absolutistic answer to the question was provided in 1931, when Mabel V. Morphett and Carleton Washburne of the highly respected Winnetka, Illinois, school system concluded that a child with a mental age of 6.5 is ready to read (22). When this finding was accepted by many as the authoritative answer to a terribly complex and difficult question, all sorts of testing programs were designed to assess the mental age of children thought to be teetering on the brink of reading readiness. The Morphett-Washburne study admitted that some children with a mental age of less than six were able to progress in reading, although their number was small. At the other end of the scale, they found that very few children with mental ages between 7.5 and nine had difficulty learning to read.

The problem with this study is that it was carried out with a school population that was essentially homogeneous. In today's schools, cultural diversity is so great that measurements of mental age are not altogether reliable; the instruments are weighted against nonnative speakers of English and speakers of nonstandard English. Current tests are accurate in that those who score low on them, because of their cultural differences from mainstream American children, are often the students who have difficulty learning to read. As measures of intellectual potential, however, the tests are generally biased and, therefore, unreliable. The danger of such tests is that schools may misconstrue the meaning of the scores, making the presumption that students who have a mental age below 6.5 are not ready to read and should not receive reading instruction.

Low scores at this point can become self-fulfilling prophecies for students; they can force early categorization to occur, and set loose the very forces about which Robert Rosenthal and Lenore Jacobson have written (23)—specifically that teachers' expectations of students significantly affect the academic performance of those students. To do so would surely work to the detriment of most of the students who have been so categorized.

Recently a new tool for indicating reading readiness has been suggested by Meredyth Daneman and Adèle Blennerhassett, whose research, although far from complete or exhaustive, suggests that children's listening spans may provide clues to when they are reaching the point of reading readiness. These researchers find that "the listening span test . . . was still the best single predictor of listening comprehension, even for preschoolers" (24). They report that among the 24 children in their sample, "the 8 children with small listening spans of 1 or 1.5 sentences were correct on only 48 percent of the high-integration items [on which they were tested]; the 16 children with the larger spans of 2 to 3 sentences were correct on 77 percent of the items" (25).

Daneman and Blennerhassett conclude that "although the present study was not designed to elicit direct evidence on [the question of reading readiness], there is some promising albeit scanty evidence to suggest that listening span could indeed be used as a tool for predicting reading readiness" (26). More research is needed in this area and should soon be undertaken.

Teachers of reading should listen to Durkin's admonition that it is not necessary that children be "ready" in all the areas that constitute readiness in order for the teacher to begin reading instruction with them. "Instead, we should be thinking in terms of readiness in the sense that one collection of abilities makes a child ready for one kind of instruction, while a somewhat different collection might make him ready to cope with another." Durkin notes that it is an all too common belief that children "must be able to do everything—and right away. Such an assumption," she reminds her readers, "needs to be replaced by one which recognizes that a child learns to read, a step at a time; and that the important readiness requirement is that he is able to learn the first step." Durkin concludes her statement with perhaps the most important reminder of all: "Fortunately, success with that first step often prepares the child to be ready for the second" (27). At this point in reading instruction, success is all important. Children who have a strong sense of having accomplished something and of having been recognized for that accomplishment will be motivated to continue their accomplishments in reading—and in their minds they will probably view reading as a pleasant and rewarding activity.

READING AND WRITING

Young children begin to see and understand the relationship between the printed word and the spoken word when they start to write. Some students can actually write before they can read, as impossible as this may seem. A great deal of students' success in reading has to do with their development of what the concept *word* communicates. Shane Templeton writes, "Children's concept of 'word' develops as a consequence of (1) their exposure to print in the everyday environment and in connected text and (2) their own attempts at writing" (28).

Reading, as Sandra Stotsky says, "has usually been related to listening and writing to speaking, rather than either one to the other" (29). This situation, of course, is understandable because on the surface, at least, reading and listening are decoding processes, whereas writing and speaking are encoding processes. Nevertheless, considerable evidence is being accumulated to suggest that a relationship exists between reading and writing and that understanding this relationship can help teachers to improve instruction in both reading and writing.

It has been demonstrated that as children compose text, however simple it may be, they start to construct their own understanding of the relationship between speech and print (30). Initially, such writing will bear little resemblance to what one usually thinks of as writing. Maryann M. Manning and Gary Manning say, "In the beginning children will invent their own spellings for familiar words.... As children develop, if they are given opportunities to write frequently, their spellings of words will become more conventional" (31). Students will eventually come to understand sound-letter relationships, and this will move them toward more conventional spelling. Templeton writes: "Children do not develop their concepts about print by passively copying what they find in their environment.... Most children want to write, and will do so if given the opportunity" (32).

One researcher has found that as children learn to write their names and the names of their friends, they are being moved closer to reading readiness (33). Through writing names, they also will learn a number of letter-sound relationships that will help them ultimately with their spelling.

READINESS AND SPELLING

Donald D. Durrell has classified the letters of the alphabet according to their phonetic qualities. In composing a reading readiness test, Durrell found that among 63 children in the bottom tenth of his kindergarten distribution, "the ability to identify the first letter in these spoken words was relatively easy: *beaver, ceiling, deep, genius, people, teacher, veal,* and *zebra.* (Median success rate, 41 percent.)" However, when Durrell moved to words whose first letters were not phonetic—*ball, cold, dog, game, paint, tent, visit,* and *zoo,* the median success rate dropped to 21 percent (34), indicating that in the earliest reading instruction, the more phonetic the words are, the more likely it is that students will be able to pronounce them.

Durrell also found that in words beginning with short "e," students identified as the first letter the first phonetic letter—*f* for *effort, l* for *elephant, m* for *emerald, n* for *engine, s* for *Esther,* and *x* for *extra.*

THE PHYSICAL ASPECTS OF READINESS

Classroom teachers in kindergarten and the primary grades must be particularly observant of signs that suggest to them which students have physical problems that might interfere with their learning, particularly with their learning to read. Remember that children who have never seen clearly or have never heard well are probably unaware of having any disability. In order for people to know that their vision or hearing is inadequate, they must have some standard against which to compare it. Children who have always seen objects as fuzzy outlines or heard sounds as garbled, distant vibrations are usually unaware that anyone else sees or hears differently from the way they do.

Observant teachers can detect signs of problems and can seek help for students whom they suspect of having visual or auditory handicaps. When teachers detect problems of this sort early, many students can be treated and have their vision or hearing corrected to close to normal. As a result, such students will be better able to succeed in their school work.

Visually handicapped students may seem inattentive. They may work on something like a drawing for a short period of time and then look out the window, seeming to have lost interest in what they are doing. They may squint when they look at objects or at the chalkboard, and they may push their eyelids and eyeballs with their fingers in an attempt to sharpen the focus by altering the shape of the eyeball. Some may show physical manifestations of the problem such as tearing or redness of the eyeball or eyelids. Some may have accumulations of mucus in the corners of their eyes or on their eyelashes. They may rub their eyes a great deal, and, when they look at books, they may hold them very close, very far away, or at odd angles. They may close one eye as they try to focus on something. All these behaviors may point to visual problems, which, if unattended, will make it difficult or impossible for the child to read.

Students with hearing defects may also have difficulty developing in areas related to language. Such children may talk much less than others. Like the visually handicapped, they may seem inattentive and/or unresponsive. They may turn their better ear to the speaker or cock their head or cup their hands behind their ears. Teachers who suspect that children have hearing defects should note whether such children have visible discharges from either or both ears. Also, teachers might ask such children to play a radio or phonograph, paying close attention to the amount of volume such children select in order to hear what is being played.

Some schools routinely examine children for visual and auditory acuity. In schools where this policy is not in force, teachers must be vigilant to see that any handicapped students are identified and helped. Even where examinations are routinely given, teachers should report anything that might have been overlooked in the routine examination because visual and auditory defects not only can put children far behind in the initial learning experience but also can give them a psychological disadvantage that may remain for a lifetime.

43

FACTORS THAT AFFECT READINESS

Class size can have an enormous effect on how well a child is able to read. Jack A. Holmes has examined thoroughly the question of class size and concludes that the younger the student, the more desirable it is to have small classes. He contends that if children are to be taught at the kindergarten level (age five or below), a student-teacher ratio of 10 to 1 is the absolute maximum. He writes, "Other things being equal, the earliest age at which a child can be taught to read is a function of the amount of time or help the teacher can give the pupil" (35). School districts are sometimes penny-wise and pound-foolish in staffing policies. Rather than achieving the desired ratio at the kindergarten or primary level, they later employ remedial reading teachers to try to salvage the students who might have learned to read in the primary grades had more personal attention been available to them at that point in their education.

An important social variable affecting reading instruction is that boys and girls at age six or seven are not equal in maturity. F. L. Ilg and L. B. Ames write about youngsters who are old enough, both mentally and chronologically, to enter first grade but who lack the maturity to succeed at the tasks required of first grade students. The researchers call these youngsters the "superior immatures" (36). The majority of students so designated are boys; because boys and girls normally enter school at the same chronological age, the difference in gender can have a profound impact on the learning situation in the primary grades.

Jeanette Jansky and Katrina de Hirsch find that "Most studies report that girls are ready to read earlier than are boys and that they retain this advantage through the lower grades" (37). They go on to cite several convincing studies to support their contentions, including one study whose conclusion is that at age six, boys are a full year behind girls in skeletal development! (38)

Most experienced teachers realize the difference in the maturity of boys and girls; these differences present teaching problems on a continuing basis. Most boys do not catch up to girls in maturity until puberty so that the differences last well into junior high school or middle school.

One solution to the problem would be to allow girls to enter first grade at an earlier age than boys are permitted to enter. Because boys eventually do catch up, however, this solution is not feasible. The more obvious solution is to provide for individual differences by reducing the student-teacher ratios in the lower grades. If this solution seems economically impractical, certainly the alternatives available are even more so.

TESTING FOR READINESS

Readiness tests abound. The most commonly used are the *Gates Reading Readiness Test*, the *Gates-MacGinite Reading Tests: Readiness Skills*, the *Metropolitan Achievement Test*, the *Bender Visual-Motor Gestalt Test*, the *Pintner-Cunningham Primary Mental Test*, the *Wepman Auditory Discrimination Test*, and the *Lee-Clark Reading Readiness Test*. Also in common use are the *Harrison-Stroud Reading Readiness Profiles*, the *Murphy-Durrell Reading Readiness Analysis*, the *American School Reading Readiness Test*, the *Clymer-Barrett Prereading Battery*, the *Delco Readiness Test*, the *Dominion Tests*, and the *Lippincott Reading Readiness Test*.

Harris indicates that most readiness tests are concerned with three or more of the following measures:

1. Visual perception; matching of pictures, geometrical forms, letters, and words
2. Verbal comprehension, including vocabulary and concepts, sentence comprehension, and following directions
3. Auditory perception, including recognizing whether whole words are the same or different, recognizing rhyming sounds, or finding words with similar initial consonant sounds
4. The ability to identify letters of the alphabet and digits
5. Sample lessons, in which a small number of words are taught by a specified procedure for a specified length of time, after which the ability to recognize the words is tested
6. Rating scales for teachers to use in rating the children on characteristics not tested in the objective subtests
7. The ability to draw or to copy a drawing. (39)

It is of the utmost importance that readiness tests be introduced in an informal, gamelike atmosphere. Students should not feel threatened by such tests, nor should they ever have the sense that their only alternatives are to pass or to fail.

STARTING EARLY

Opinions are sharply divided on the question of how much encouragement should be given children to begin reading early. Certainly many talented children have begun reading at phenomenally early ages. Clarence Darrow, the famed attorney, reminisces: "I cannot remember when

45

I learned to read. I seem always to have known how. I am sure that I learned my letters from the red and blue books that were always scattered on the floor. . . . It must be that my father gave me little chance to tarry long from one single book to another, for I remember that at a very early age, I was told again and again that John Stuart Mill began studying Greek when he was only three years old" (40). Another prodigy, Norbert Weiner, the famed mathematician who earned a doctorate before his twenty-first year, reports that he was fully able to read at the age of five and "had full liberty to roam in what was the very catholic and miscellaneous library of my father" (41).

Durkin has suggested that early exposure to reading instruction might give slower students a needed head start: "Children of relatively lower intelligence especially benefit from an early start . . . it might well [be] that slower children need contact with learning to read that is spread out over time" (42). Notable experiments in Whitby, Connecticut, and in Denver, Colorado, have demonstrated that children can be taught the physical act of reading earlier than is usually the case. The question is whether this is the most efficient long-term procedure. While much research remains to be done in the field, some early findings suggest that starting children too early may result in a cycle of failure that impedes their future learning. The much-cited study by George D. Spache and others (43) reports that the children in the two lowest quartiles of the study whose reading program was begun in January or March scored higher on reading tests at the end of the year than did comparable students who had been introduced to reading instruction in the preceding September or November.

WHAT TEACHERS CAN DO

Kindergarten and primary teachers should not push their students into reading. Nevertheless, they should build the best reading environment possible within their own classrooms. Language in all its manifestations should be used constantly: stories should be told; dramas should be enacted; books and other attractive reading materials should be abundant; posters should be displayed; items such as desks, chairs, tables, walls, windows, erasers, and plants should be labeled in block letters (44).

Teachers should note whether any students can read fluently from books around the room. Can these students read silently as well as orally? Can they recognize words from the stories they read when the words are isolated? Can they read words in lower-case as well as upper-case letters when they are printed on cards? Can they differentiate among such letters as *b*, *d*, *p*, and *g*? Among *h*, *m*, *n*, and *u*? Among *C*, *D*, *G,* and *O*? Do they sound their vowels in such a way that there is a differentiation among *pan*, *pen*, and *pin*? Among *tan*, *ten*, and *tin*?

Teachers should encourage students to tell them stories that they then print in block letters on sheets of paper. Students often begin reading with relative ease if it is their own stories that they are reading. They also enjoy reading stories that other students in the class have told to the teacher. After such stories are written by the teacher (and they may be only a sentence or two long at the beginning), students should be encouraged to copy their stories in block letters resembling those the teacher has used.

The most important and reassuring strategy that can help to prepare students to read is the natural introduction of print media of all sorts into the classroom. Such media should be introduced into game situations; for example, playing store, which involves reading labels and dealing with play money, will enhance the early reading skills of young students.

The skillful teacher of young children will work to bring them to the point of wanting to read and will then carefully pilot them through the shoals to the point at which they read to satisfy their curiosity and needs.

Chapter 5
HOW COMPUTERS HELP CHILDREN LEARN TO READ

Most schools have been caught up in the computer revolution of the 1980s. No level of education has been left untouched by this revolution, and the future of all instruction is now as intimately related to it as it generally has been to the use of textbooks. Students in elementary schools are active members of the computer generation, and already many seven- or eight-year-old youngsters are far more computer literate than both their parents and their teachers. Conscientious teachers are working strenuously to learn as much as they can about computers and to prepare instructional materials appropriate to computerized instruction.

Computers offer teachers and students many advantages, not the least of which are that computers have infinite patience and that they offer immediate feedback. Educators have for decades recommended that teachers give students as much individual attention as they can, and dedicated teachers, usually handicapped by large class enrollments, have universally experienced considerable frustration at not being able to give their students more individualized instruction and individual attention. The use of computers has remedied this situation substantially and has led to greatly improved learning outcomes for students at all age levels and of all abilities.

OVERCOMING THE FEAR OF COMPUTERS

Not surprisingly, many teachers feel grossly inadequate to deal with the computer revolution, which has burst upon them almost overnight. Microcomputers demand exact commands and will not respond when the commands contain even slight variations from prescribed form, such as a misplaced slash mark or asterisk. Teachers who have had the bulb on the film projector burn out at the dramatic moment when 25 lively students have been primed to watch a film or who have had mimeograph fluid leak out of its drum all over their papers, their clothing, and the workroom floor have an understandable distrust of machines. To them, the microcomputer may seem more awesome than the film projector or the mimeograph machine because the microcomputer seems almost able to think and because its programs place users in an interactive relationship that is much more sophisticated than the interaction one normally has with other machines.

The only way to overcome computerphobia, a perfectly legitimate malady of the 1980s, is to plunge right in and begin to use a microcomputer. Teachers whose school districts offer them the opportunity to buy microcomputers at reduced prices and to pay for them with interest-free, payroll deduction loans are cheating themselves and their students if they do not take advantage of this opportunity.

For the first week or two, new computer owners will probably be overwhelmed by what they need to learn. Most computer manuals are bewildering at first, confusing and frustrating most users. Since reading the whole manual will probably be counterproductive at this point, it is best initially to find out from the manual how to boot the machine—that is, how to get it to the point that it will receive and dispense information—and then to work from there.

Begin to read beyond the computer manual, focusing on articles that deal with the uses of computers as they relate to teaching reading. *The Reading Teacher* has offered a steady flow of such articles, and George Mason has also done much through his monthly column, "The Printout," to inform teachers of the possibilities that exist for using microcomputers on a daily basis in classrooms. *Mindstorms: Children, Computers, and Powerful Ideas* (1) is an exciting book by Seymour Papert, a mathematician from the Massachusetts Institute of Technology who spent five years in Geneva studying with Piaget. Papert shows how students of varying ability and age levels can use the computer to help them gain mastery over the basic skills they need as well as to move on to the more sophisticated skills of high-level reasoning. In a recent issue of *English Journal*, this writer has suggested a dozen ways in which teachers can use microcomputers in their classrooms, dividing this list into administrative uses, instructional uses, and combined administrative and instructional uses (2).

It is helpful at this stage in your transition to computer user to find colleagues who are a little more advanced in using computers than you are and who don't mind receiving a desperate call for help occasionally. Try out various computer programs, and if you don't get the desired results, turn to the manual and turn to friends who are willing to help. User groups have formed in most cities, and if you become affiliated with such a group, you will find that the members are supportive and generous in giving help.

If you do not have your own microcomputer, start using those available at your school. Use the computer at first to keep records of student performance since you have to do this housekeeping job in one way or another anyway. Begin by creating a file for each student in which you record information about grades, classroom reports, group activities, and other elements of student performance. You should always copy your important files onto a back-up disk so that if the original disk should be damaged in any way, you will still have the information. And do not let the last statement frighten you. I have been using the microcomputer for two years now, and I have yet to lose any information from any of the dozens of disks I have filed. Nevertheless, knowing that I have a back-up for the important ones makes it easier for me to sleep at night.

After a week of experimenting with the computer, you should begin to gain confidence, although you will still experience some frustrations and will make some mistakes. By the end of two weeks, you probably will begin to wonder how you lived before the microcomputer began to take the drudgery out of so many elements of your professional life.

LEARNING MORE ABOUT COMPUTERS AND READING INSTRUCTION

Most libraries are now awash in new books and periodicals about computers and education. The International Reading Association has published *Computer Applications in Reading* by George Mason, Jay S. Blanchard, and Danny B. Daniel (3). This book is essential for teachers who want to use computers for reading instruction. Its suggestions are practical, and although any computer book is dated before its distribution because the field is expanding so rapidly, the information in this book is of sufficient general usefulness that it will be valuable for some years to come. Also of as enduring value as any book in this field can be is Leo Geoffrion and Olga Geoffrion's *Computers and Reading Instruction* (4). Although one needs constant updates on software, these two books provide useful guidelines for evaluating software. They also suggest literally scores of ways in which computers can be used to enhance reading instruction at various grade levels, and the Geoffrion's book has the best list presently available of software one can use in teaching reading.

The Center for the Study of Reading (CSR) at the University of Illinois (51 Gerty Drive, Champaign, IL 61820) produces regular research reports that are aimed at teachers and administrators rather than at researchers and that focus considerable attention on possible classroom applications of these research findings. Quarterly lists of their reports are available on request, and copies of the actual reports are available through ERIC or, for a nominal fee, directly from CSR. Of particular interest is *Reading and Writing with Computers* (CSR Reading Education Report No. 42).

SCHOOL COMPUTERS

If your school has not yet entered the computer age, it is in the minority. You and your colleagues should make the best case you can for the purchase of at least two microcomputers for every elementary school classroom, although one computer for every five students would be the desirable ratio. The school should also have extra computers that can be loaned to teachers who are planning lessons that require more than the usual number of machines. Having extra machines also should assure uninterrupted instruction when a classroom machine is out of commission and needs servicing.

Most schools have made significant headway in equipping classrooms with computers. Once the initial move is made, teachers and administrators realize what an indispensable learning tool the microcomputer is, and they become evangelists for the purchase of additional machines and the software to run them.

Regardless of the grade level at which you are teaching, you can count on having some students who know more about how to operate microcomputers than you do, and, with their help, you should be able to put your machines to immediate use. When you begin to use them, you will realize that computer users can either control or be controlled by the machines. It is important pedagogically to acknowledge this situation and to guide each student into the sort of relationship with the microcomputer that seems appropriate.

The rest of this chapter will suggest ways in which computers can be used effectively in various learning situations involving the teaching of reading. Most of the suggestions are easy to implement, and they provide the kind of individualized instruction that we only dreamed of until the computer revolution overtook the schools in the early 1980s.

COMPUTER ASSISTED READING

Microcomputers can serve many functions in the teaching of reading at the elementary school level. They can be especially valuable to stu-

51

dents in the upper elementary grades who are not good readers. Such students may view books as symbols of their earlier failures and will make better progress in their reading if they deal with print in contexts other than the book.

Patricia N. Chrosniak and George W. McConkie have conducted pilot studies with elementary school students who read below grade level and have devised a Computer Assisted Reading (CAR) program. Their program presents a text on the screen which the students read. The students are equipped with light pens, and whenever they come to an unfamiliar word, they touch the word with the pen. The computer is programmed through an audio recording to articulate any word that is touched. The Chrosniak-McConkie program is so designed that whenever a word is touched with the light pen, it is not only articulated but also intensified on the screen so that the reader's attention is drawn to it. The program stores up to 3,000 words and can deliver any one of them in articulated form in half a second.

The researchers reasoned that if children are reading in informal contexts at home and come to words they do not know, they can ask whoever is there what the unfamiliar word is and, once having been told the word, can go on with their reading. Many beginning readers achieve a fair reading speed when they receive this sort of assistance. Chrosniak and McConkie speculated that if the computer were programmed to give the same sort of assistance that a parent or older sibling might give in an informal setting, beginning readers would more readily develop better reading habits and an increased enthusiams for reading than if they had to struggle with every unfamiliar word. Also, because their reading speed would increase, their comprehension of the material they were reading should increase as well.

In order that students could move as quickly as possible into substantively interesting reading material, Chrosniak and McConkie presented students with reading material two grade levels above the level at which they were reading. To give students books so far beyond their reading levels would in most conventional situations be to invite discouragement and frustration. However, because students using the Chrosniak-McConkie program have immediate help with every word that gives them difficulty, they begin to read quite easily from the advanced materials presented to them.

The researchers found that even students who had to use their light pens extensively for help understood the passages they were reading. They report, ''Tape recordings made of the children reading aloud in early and final sessions clearly demonstrate the change in reading fluency that took place as the children learned to use the computer's help'' (5). Also, of course, when this sort of reading assistance is available, students will gain a familiarity with words they do not know initially and will increase their sight vocabularies.

All of the students in the Chrosniak-McConkie study were from the third, fourth and fifth grades, and their reading levels were from 8 to 27 months below grade level. The Distar reading program was used with these youngsters. The study extended over a 10-week period, with each student reading for 20 to 30 minutes a day, five days a week. They were exposed to a broad variety of reading materials ranging from fables, folk tales, and children's stories to essays, biographies, and human interest stories.

The children were given the *Woodcock Reading Mastery Test* before and after the study, and each child was tested for decoding ability and spelling recognition. Because students neither spent enormous amounts of time trying to sound out unfamiliar words nor skipped over them, their comprehension of the material they read increased substantially. One might also speculate that a program like CAR could lead students to become independent readers more quickly than conventional reading instruction is able to.

LEARNING THE KEYBOARD

If students receive formal instruction in touch typing, it is usually at the secondary level. However, with the ascendancy of microcomputers in schools, it now is desirable for students to learn touch typing earlier. Also, whereas touch typing has generally been taught to students in commercial programs and to a small number of students who elect the beginning course in typing, current wisdom indicates that probably all students should receive some formal instruction in the skill so that they can gain familiarity with the computer keyboard.

Some elementary school students have received instruction in touch typing as far back as 1895 (6), and special courses in the skill have been available to students in the 6- to 12-year age range in a small number of schools around the country for the last three or four decades. Many of these courses have been offered in special summer enrichment programs. The available data indicate that students who take such courses have shown gains in their reading and writing abilities as they have learned to type. Their spelling, grammar, and punctuation generally improved as they became better typists (7).

J. L. Rowe reports on a summer course in touch typing given to third and fourth grade students. The students who completed the course increased four months on standardized tests of their reading comprehension levels and seven months in their vocabulary levels. The control group of students who were not involved in any summer school activity lost a month in their reading comprehension levels and three months in their vocabulary levels in the same period (8). Students in Fort Lauderdale and Stuart, Florida, who learned touch typing in special elementary school classes showed considerable progress. In standard measurements of their abilities, more than half of them tested one year ahead of students who had not taken touch typing (9).

Certainly the hunt-and-peck method of using the keyboard of the microcomputer is inefficient. Students should be weaned from it as soon as they have the motor skills they need to learn to type. The instruction they receive should not be as concentrated as in a typing course at the secondary school level. The computer is more forgiving than conventional typewriters so the degree of perfection in typing that was once required need no longer be demanded.

Students who have been using microcomputers in the primary grades are likely to have a head start on learning the keyboard, even if they are still hunt-and-peck typists. They are unlikely to require more than a few weeks of instruction, probably in 20- to 30-minute increments (10), in order to learn enough touch typing to serve their needs in using microcomputers. Students should not be pushed into instruction in touch typing, but such instruction should be available to them when they show an interest in learning how to type.

COMPUTERS AND STORY TELLING

Story telling has long been recognized as a fundamental part of reading instruction in the early elementary grades. In the past, teachers sometimes copied stories on large sheets of paper as students told them and then used these stories as a resource for teaching reading to the rest of the class.

The microcomputer permits teachers in the early grades to go a step beyond the former method by typing the stories students tell in class into the computer and then making printouts of these stories. The advantage of using such material is that it will usually be in the dialect of many of the youngsters in class as well as being at their reading levels. Once students' stories are on diskettes, the students who composed them can work at revising them, expanding them, and making them more effective.

Mark Grabe and Cindy Grabe recommend that teachers copy the stories that students present orally so that "children gain firsthand experience with writing/reading relationships by learning to read stories they have written. They can extend these insights by learning to read stories dictated by friends" (11). This approach helps students in the class to interact and to share ideas with each other. It can also lead to effective group composition sessions. Once students begin to work with their stories and begin to alter them on the monitor, they will see that revision is an opportunity rather than a chore and that the challenge of turning a good piece of writing into an outstanding one is great. They will also begin to make connections between the words of the story as they have dictated it and the graphic representation of those words on the monitor or on the printout. Because they have dictated the story, they will be working with familiar vocabulary, and the burden of decoding should be lighter than it would be if they were reading stories printed in a book. Also, the decoding should be less mechanical, more rhythmical than it typically is when students read aloud sentences someone else has written.

Curtis C. Dudley-Marling suggests that when teachers use microcomputers essentially for drill and practice, which certainly can be carried out well on them, their students' language experience may become fragmented, whereas when teachers employ microcomputers for such activities as recording students' stories, "there is some evidence that using computers may result in longer language experience stories and more revisions" (12). Dudley-Marling also suggests that students' stories stored on a diskette might be followed by cloze sentences drawn from the stories that will indicate students comprehension of what they are reading. He contends, too, that students who use microcomputers as word processors will be more likely to take risks in their writing than will students who compose their stories in a less flexible medium. The microcomputer not only makes revision easy but also makes it possible for students to structure their stories in numerous ways before deciding on a final version.

Nancy J. Smith reaches conclusions similar to Dudley-Marling's. She writes, "The search/replace capability [of microcomputers] encourages synonym substitution and the immediate access to a clean copy stimulates further language play" (13). The old system under which students learned to read and write encouraged neatness, sometimes at the expense of quality. The microcomputer permits both neatness and quality.

INTERACTIVE STORY TELLING

Human creativity is more pronounced in most children's preliterate years than at any other time in their lives, and teachers in the primary grades have a special responsibility to keep this creativity and imagination alive. With the help of the microcomputer, they can use prepackaged interactive stories with their students, or they can create interactive stories themselves and put them on diskettes.

An interactive story is one in which the reader (the user of the microcomputer) helps to decide the story's outcome. At various crucial points in the story, users are given options from which to choose. The option they select at a given point will determine how the story will unfold up to the next crucial point, where other options will be provided.

Interactive stories heighten students awareness of story structure because they must exercise their options at structurally significant points in the story (14). Recent research reveals that students who are aware of the structure of texts read those texts with greater comprehension than do those students who are not aware of textual structure (15). Interactive stories introduced in the primary grades not only fascinate most students but also help them to develop an awareness of literary structure that will ultimately help them to become more sensitive and efficient readers as they move into the upper elementary and middle grades.

Grabe and Grabe, who have had experience in creating interactive stories, recommend that students work on them in groups and put them on diskettes after working out their stories on paper. The Grabes emphasize that the group-constructed stories "should center on student experience and interest" (16). They have had success in using this activity just before the Christmas holiday, encouraging groups of students to invent stories about something connected with the holiday season.

Few techniques work better to stimulate the imaginations and the inventive faculties of young students than to engage in working with interactive stories and then, when they have begun to understand how these stories work, to engage them in group activities that result in their producing new interactive stories. The stories they produce will generally have the advantage of being at the interest and maturity levels of the other students in the class.

USING COMPUTERS STORIES AND GAMES
TO ENCOURAGE READING

If reading is to become a pleasurable pursuit, it must provide outcomes for the reader. The verb *to read* is generally a transitive verb—that is, it takes an object. We do not just read; we read something.

To say that someone likes to read is probably a misstatement or, at least, an incomplete statement. People who like to read would presumably be as happy to read the telephone directory from cover to cover as they would be to read a novel or a how-to-do-it book or a daily newspaper. Common sense tells us that few such people exist. Avid readers are not avid readers because they continually practice their skills in isolation—they use their reading skills to read something that interests and informs them. Primary school students who are subjected to reading materials that do not interest and inform them—the Dick and Jane type of story is extremely limited in its ability to hold the interest of even the most docile youngsters—may develop an early antipathy toward reading, especially now when most three- and four-year-old youngsters are used to receiving colorful and exciting information from television.

Roger Farr chides teachers who contend that they are trying to make their students love to read. He is clear in stating, "We should be teaching reading so that children learn that reading is one more avenue to help them do and enjoy those things they want to do and enjoy." He continues: "We can teach children to love making things, finding out about new ideas, and enjoying a variety of experiences, but we cannot teach them to love reading. Reading is a means to an end, not an end in itself" (17). Too often teachers bent on getting their students to decode lose sight of the highest purposes of reading.

Farr responds to parental questions about why time in school is wasted on playing games and doing projects. He writes, "These loaded questions may come from parents who have not yet taken the time to sit down with their children to discover that they are reading to complete the games and projects" (18). He urges that "learning to read should involve children in experiences that they enjoy and that demonstrate that reading is a way to gain information, to solve problems, to encounter ideas, and to be entertained. This involves the teacher in identifying real reasons for children to read. Reading is the comprehension and subsequent use of ideas" (19).

Now that many elementary school classrooms are equipped with computers, teachers can make excellent use of computer games that require the players to read. Dudley-Marling suggests that reading must be done for real purposes or else it will be taught as a fragmented (and meaningless) set of skills. He identifies available programs that meet the ends of reading teachers (20) and suggests in particular Tom Snyder's *Snooper Troops* (Cambridge, MA: Spinnaker Software, 1982), *Dragon's Keep* by Al Lowe and others (Coarsegold, CA: Sierra On-Line Systems, 1983), Mary Blank's *Deadline*, (Cambridge, MA: Inforcom, 1982), and *Window on Learning: The Learning Magazine on a Disk* (Watertown, MA: Window, 1983).

Snooper Troops is a collection of mysteries that require players to follow written clues and to test hypotheses. It certainly engages players not only in reading but also in developing some reasoning skills.

Dragon's Keep is an easy game appropriate for use with some preschool and primary grade children. The user's task is to search a building and set some animals within the building free. The vocabulary is simple, but the interest level is high. Many of the clues are one-word clues, and even those that are presented in phrases are within the grasp of beginning readers if they have a teacher available to help them.

Deadline differs from *Snooper Troops* and *Dragon's Keep* in that it is a novel that involves the reader directly in charting the course of the story. The decisions the reader makes will determine the outcome of the story. Students who have developed a degree of independence in reading will like the control they can assert over the novel as they work through the program and as they interact with it.

Window on Learning, the most varied of the four programs, contains a variety of games, articles, puzzles, and simulations, much as *Scholastic Magazine* does—but this entire magazine is on a disk with which students can interact. The disk holds a variety of activities at different ability levels so that it is a serviceable program to use in the classroom.

In many students, reading skills will develop almost automatically if they are exposed to exciting computer programs that demand reading. The combination of pictures and words in interactive computer programs is often a more effective way of teaching students to read than is the use of books, although one should not displace the other.

SPELLING AND THE MICROCOMPUTER

Microcomputers offer significant help to students in word recognition and spelling. Initially, students can be shown a picture and then be asked to supply the missing letter of a word pertaining to that picture. A picture of a cat would have beneath it __ AT. If the student provided "C," the response would be acknowledged as a correct one. If the student pressed the wrong letter, let us say "H," or pressed the return to indicate that he or she did not know the letter, the correct word would flash on the screen. The student could then try the exercise again.

The microcomputer can be programmed to present the word with a different missing letter once the student indicates correctly the first letter: for example, with the word *CAT*, the student would go from __ AT to C __ T to CA __. Finally, the student might be asked to type the word relating to the picture with no letters provided.

Once students have mastered a vocabulary of a few nouns they can spell correctly, the program can be designed so that when they type a word on the screen, a picture will appear depicting the noun that was typed. As students work through the program, they gain increasing mastery over the microcomputer and develop the sense of being able to make it do things for them.

With the development of their spelling ability, students also develop their reading skills because they are forced to make the kinds of word/ picture associations and discriminations that are fundamental parts of reading. The microcomputer also has the advantage of being able to keep records on the progress of the students using it and, on the basis of these records, is able to repeat drills for individual students when it seems appropriate to do so. Computers can also analyze data and lead teachers to useful generalizations about the kinds of spelling problems that individual students have. This kind of immediate diagnosis permits teachers to focus and individualize their teaching as they have never been able to do in the past.

If students spell a word correctly, the microcomputer can be programmed to highlight that correct spelling so that they can fix on it visually and can grow used to seeing how the word looks when it is spelled correctly (21). It can also drill students in words they have missed in previous sessions.

As students become more proficient and as they begin to compose pieces, they can use a spelling program, available with most word processing programs (22), to check their work. Running these checks can provide excellent instruction in spelling because the user must correct misspelled words. Some programs, such as Wordperfect 4.1, have the capability of providing correct spelling alternatives for the words that are misspelled.

COMPUTERS AND RESEARCH IN READING

The computer has opened to reading researchers possibilities that were unheard of even a decade ago. Modern computers can be programmed to gather all sorts of data about students who are engaged in experimental programs. The computer, for example, has been used to measure eye movements in reading with such detail that researchers are beginning to change their views on such questions as when students should first be introduced to reading (23).

George W.McConkie, David Zola, and N. Roderick Underwood have recently been engaged in extensive research studies concerning eye movement. Their computerized measurement of eye movements shows that at early ages, some children cannot focus sufficiently on printed letters to be able to read (24). If children are encouraged to read at this stage of their development, which is different for every child, they will not be up to the task physically and will fail at it. This failure can be significant because it will make reading an unpleasant experience for such children, an experience they will come to associate with failure. By the time they have the visual coordination to permit them to read, they may be turned off to reading and may be on the road to becoming nonreaders.

Research of this sort, validated by the computer, makes one realize that hazards lurk in the notion that reading should be taught to all kindergarten or all first grade children. Probably children should not be graded for the first three years of elementary school; rather they should simply be in a primary classroom in which they are surrounded by opportunities for learning to read, but are not pushed into reading. Those who are not ready to read will engage in nonreading activities and will be encouraged to read by being read to or by engaging in paired reading (25). As their interest in their stories grows, they can engage in composition through telling stories that the teacher will record. In time, they will begin to read their own stories with pleasure, then those of their classmates, and finally those in books.

EVALUATING SOFTWARE

Software is being produced so rapidly that some teachers are overwhelmed by how much of it is available. The best way to keep up with the software explosion is at least to scan such professional journals as *The Reading Teacher, Journal of Reading, Language Arts,* and *English Jour-*

nal on a regular basis. A great deal of software is reviewed in their pages. While these reviews are often brief, they cover a large amount of computer software. For example, Judy Wedman has written a two-page article that reports on her review of 43 catalogs from educational publishers. She lists the 19 that contain software advertisements and then catalogs the material according to the skills they emphasize, after which she makes useful generalizations about the material (26).

Your school or local public library will probably have some of the following magazines that focus on microcomputers and review available software:

A+
Audiovisual Instruction
BYTE
Centurion News
Classroom Computer Learning
Classroom Computer News
Compute!
Computers and Education
Computers, Reading & Language Arts
Computer World
Courseware
Creative Computing
Educational Computer Magazine
Educational Technology
Electronic Learning
Infoworld
Instructional Innovator

Macworld
Media and Methods
Microcomputers in Education
PC
PC World
Personal Computing
Popular Computing
School Courseware Journal
School Microware Reviews
Softalk
Softside
Software News
SYNC
Teaching and Computers
Video Magazine
Video Review

In addition, individual companies including IBM, Apple, and Texas Instruments issue journals that deal with their machines. These journals are readily available in most stores that sell magazines.

If your school has computers, it probably buys software on a regular basis, and you should try to devote at least one hour a week to reviewing some of the new programs that have come in. Ernest Balajthy suggests that when reviewing simulation software, teachers should ask certain questions (27)—and actually many of the questions he proposes are applicable to software other than that devoted to simulations. Among the questions one might ask are the following, which are based on Balajthy's suggestions and are adapted to the more general purposes of reading teachers:

1. Does the software involve language activities?
2. Does the program teach valuable concepts, appropriate to the students with whom I will be using it?
3. Can related printed reading materials be used effectively to supplement the program?
4. Does the publisher provide teaching aids?
5. Are the variables presented appropriate to my students?
6. Does the program present any random variables?
7. Does the program use graphics? If so, are they intelligently related to the program?

A WORD ABOUT TEACHER ATTITUDE

Major changes in teaching techniques may be threatening to people who have been doing things in a given way and have enjoyed a modicum of success in doing it thus. The microcomputer, which in many instances takes attention away from the teacher as the central figure in the classroom, in some instances makes the teacher more of a manager than an instructor. While this shift in emphasis can arouse apprehension, if teachers once begin to use microcomputers, they will soon discover whole new worlds of teaching possibilities.

Teachers who refuse to use microcomputers will be the dinosaurs of our age, and their students will be significantly shortchanged. To get started, one must have a moderate spirit of adventure and must be willing to endure a week or two of frustration before he or she gains enough control over the instrument to feel comfortable using it. When this day arrives, the turning point has been reached, and the new user will start to become an evangelist for microcomputers. This is a certainty.

Chapter 6
THE LANGUAGE EXPERIENCE APPROACH TO TEACHING READING

THE LANGUAGE EXPERIENCE APPROACH (LEA) DEFINED

The Language Experience Approach (LEA) to teaching reading is essentially what its name implies—an approach that capitalizes on students' experiences and, from them, draws the materials from which they will learn to read. Students, sometimes singly but more usually in groups, are encouraged to discuss topics that interest them. The teacher and/or teacher aides listen carefully as free-ranging discussions develop. Through sensitive listening, they are able to isolate topics that interest students. Then they begin to direct attention to these topics, and from them, they construct a story as the child or the group tells it, using the children's own words. The children talk, and the teacher or aide writes down some of what they say in the form of a coherent narrative.

Teachers might find that their students talk about games they play, about their pets, about their parents, about something they have seen—a television show, a movie, or a sports event—or about something they have done—made a drawing, gone on a trip, learned how to ride a bicycle, or ridden on a pony.

The teacher will then begin to question the child or group about one of the topics, preferably having already written in large block letters on large pieces of cardboard such words as "MY PUPPY," "SESAME STREET," "GOING TO SEE MY FRIEND PLAY BASEBALL," or "MY PONY RIDE." The student or students decide which topic they want to use to construct their story. As they tell what happened, the teacher or aide writes down sentences they are articulating related to the topic. Short, complete sentences are recorded in large block letters on large pieces of paper or cardboard. A typical story might look like this:

MY PONY RIDE

MY MOMMY AND DADDY TOOK ME TO A FARM.
THERE WERE PONIES ON THE FARM.
THE FARMER SAID, "DO YOU WANT TO RIDE A PONY?"
I SAID, "YES."

THE PONY'S NAME WAS SPORT.
I RODE SPORT IN THE FIELD.
I LIKE TO RIDE PONIES.

Ideally, this would be a wall story—that is, it would be displayed on a wall of the classroom so that everyone could see it. Some students might wish to illustrate their stories with drawings. Some story ideas might be derived from photographs that the students or the teacher provides.

Students who are just learning to read, regardless of their ages, should be surrounded by all sorts of printed material, ranging from picture books to catalogs to booklets made from former students' dictated stories. Their own stories should be displayed and teachers or aides should read their stories along with them; the students will probably "read" from memory in the early stages, but as they do so, they will be learning that words in print have meaning and that they can tell other people things they would like them to know through the medium of print.

A substantial body of research indicates that prereaders do not look upon words as important units (1). Once they come to realize that words are conveyers of information, however, they will have moved one step closer to being able to read. Gradually making the connection between words and ideas will make most of them more eager to learn how to read than they had previously been.

LEA has been particularly effective in teaching middle school and adult nonreaders to read. However, LEA can be used successfully at all levels of early reading instruction because it is real to students. It deals not with hypothetical people the way basal readers must, but with the students themselves. Not only are the stories theirs but, more importantly, so are the words. The vocabulary level should present fewer problems than one sometimes encounters using basal readers because the vocabulary of the stories is the vocabulary of the children telling them.

THE BEGINNINGS OF LEA

The Language Experience Approach to reading was instituted as a formal program by Roach Van Allen. During the 1950s, Allen was teaching in Harlingen, Texas, on the Mexican border, where he dealt with large numbers of students who had the problems often associated with nonnative speakers of English. Allen realized that these students had reading problems because their life experiences and language experiences had been quite unlike those of typical American students, the kinds of students at whom most textbooks were aimed at that time. Using the LEA approach, which had already been tried experimentally in the Laboratory School of the University of Chicago 30 years before, Allen found that his students made much greater progress than they had in the past.

When Allen moved from Harlingen to the San Diego Public Schools as Director of Curriculum Coordination, he found that the children in this district had many of the problems he had noticed in his Texas students. Allen instituted an LEA program in the San Diego elementary schools, particularly in the first grade. He described and explained his program in the following way:

What I can think about, I can say.
What I can say, I can write or someone can write it for me.
I can read what I have written or what someone else has written for me.
I can read what others have written for me to read. (2)

This brief statement contains the essence of the Language Experience Approach to reading instruction.

SOME CRITICISMS OF LEA

Some critics have faulted LEA because it does not teach phonic analysis and because it is relatively unstructured. Such critics apparently ignore the possibility of using LEA as an element in reading instruction rather than as an all-consuming program that precludes all other approaches. Certainly teachers can use LEA even if they are teaching reading through the use of the highly structured basal readers.

First-year teachers who are somewhat unsure of themselves may find the lack of structure in LEA a problem, and they would be well advised to begin with a more structured program and to enhance it by moving gradually into LEA. Teachers who are not comfortable with what they are doing are unlikely to do it well so they certainly should not have LEA imposed upon them administratively.

A quite real limitation of LEA is that teachers must spend considerable time transcribing children's stories. These transcriptions are generally short, but writing them out undeniably takes time. If teachers have groups work on stories, they will have less material to transcribe. They can also use teacher's aides to help in the transcribing, and sometimes parents will volunteer a few hours a week to promote this activity.

SOME ADVANTAGES OF LEA

Jeaneatte Veatch has identified the chief advantage of LEA: "Children speak and talk before they read or write. Therefore, the shortcut to reading is through their own speaking and listening" (3). The authenticity of narratives recorded as children tell them and the appropriateness of these narratives to individual children's interests and vocabulary levels recommend LEA beyond any other method of initial reading instruction, even though it should probably not be the only method of instruction in first grade. With older students and with nonreading adults, it probably can be the sole method of instruction in some cases.

Barbara Mallon and Roberta Berglund claim that LEA "motivates students to want to read and effectively demonstrates the connection between spoken and written language." They also claim that "the use of a student's own language and background of experiences encourages acquisition of a reading vocabulary as well as a comprehension of the printed word" (4). They have set up a sequential program that leads into LEA, and they provide particularly useful suggestions for teachers to follow in editing the stories for transcription. They urge that stories be kept short and simple.

Elaine Vilscek's research, conducted with first grade students, revealed that students taught by LEA in first grade had higher second grade scores overall than did those taught by other methods (5), but it also revealed that these students had a greater range of scores, so it is apparent that LEA is not the best method for all students. Vilscek found that students who came from advantaged home situations in which family members were articulate scored considerably higher than students who came from less favored circumstances.

Greater language gains are made by students in LEA during the first grade than by students who are taught reading by other means, according to Douglas E. Giles (6). Harry T. Hahn finds that students taught by LEA are superior to those who have been taught through the use of basal readers "in spelling, word recognition, and paragraph comprehension" (7). Gertrude Hildreth's research indicates that "words children use in their own speech are easier to read in print than words they do not use." She also finds that "the richness of a child's language is related to reading success" (8). Certainly LEA adds to the richness of children's language because it encourages oral communication and it enhances children's images of themselves by letting them see that their stories are important enough to be written down and displayed.

A major advantage of the Language Experience Approach is that it engages the interests of the children with whom it is used because it invokes their own experiences and uses these experiences as the bases for stories. The dialect and the vocabulary used will generally be at a level appropriate to the group from which the dictated stories come.

WHAT TO DO ABOUT DIALECTS

Teachers and researchers have been divided on the question of whether teachers should record student stories in the dialects of the students telling them. For example, if a student is telling a story about a dog and says, "My dog he be big," or, "My dog ain't got no tail," should the transcriber write the exact words or write, "My dog is big," or, "My dog doesn't have a tail"?

Veatch is unequivocal in her recommendations about this matter. She points out that children who pronounce *park* without sounding the *r* may very well be able to spell the word correctly, and are pronouncing it correctly within the limits of their own dialect. Dialectal variations such as *hock* for *hawk* and *dotter* for *daughter* are common throughout the country, and people have little trouble adjusting to them.

Veatch tells teachers: "It is, after all, quite proper for people to reflect speech patterns they have known all their lives. What is wrong with it?" She goes on to caution, "Being made to feel ashamed of how one talks is not far removed from being made to feel ashamed of one's skin color, or religion, or one's parents" (9). A great deal is said about how to deal with dialects in Chapter 10 of this book; in that chapter it is pointed out that speakers of dialects are not always in agreement with the genuinely humane sentiments of conscientious educators who want to allow students the right to their own language.

Wilma H. Miller originally shared some of Veatch's feelings about how to deal with dialects in LEA. "However, after teaching countless minority group college students, she now believes that it probably is more effective to alter very tactfully a child's dictated material to make it more nearly conform to Standard English." Miller emphasizes that "virtually all of the minority group students that I have taught have convinced me that it is absolutely imperative for all minority group children to learn how to speak and write Standard English effectively if they are going to be able to compete in our society" (10).

Both Veatch and Miller appear to be using the either/or method of reasoning rather than the both/and method. Certainly children who speak dialects significantly deviant from the norm in a community cannot begin using the dominant dialect overnight. In addressing this point, Nicholas Anastasiow says: "What a child says is only the content of his oral language. The meaning must be communicated through his word choice and sentence structure, and they depend upon the language system of his culture or subculture" (11). All children, regardless of background, must be encouraged to talk, to contribute verbally to the group activities that will lead to LEA stories.

Veatch warns that "the common opinion [is] that lower class children have nothing to talk about"; she goes on to pinpoint the origin of this false notion: "The problem is that their [lower class children's] environment is so different from other children['s] that they honestly consider themselves to come from another world and so SEEM to have nothing to say" (12). The teacher's first challenge is to get such children talking, to help make them participating members of the class. In order to do this, teachers need to know something about the dialects and the social codes that characterize the backgrounds from which their children come.

The Kamehameha Program in Hawaii, discussed in Chapter 2 of this book, has succeeded in teaching children to read by providing them with school environments that are fashioned after the home environments from which they come and that take into account the customs of the society from which the children are drawn (13). Until teachers are able to make such accommodations, some students will inevitably be dismissed as being inarticulate or slow or indifferent.

My suggestion is that the teacher who is working with students who cannot read should begin by getting all the students to talk as much as they can. Next, he or she should write down what the students have said. The teacher should then get students to read back what has been transcribed from their dictation, both their own stories and those of their classmates. Eventually, students reading someone else's story will correct that story into their own dialects. When this happens—whether the switch is from Chicano to Black, Black to Standard, Standard to Black, or any other combination—the teacher should point out the switch as a curiosity: "Now, let me see, Jenny. Jim read, 'My dog is barking,' and you read, 'My dog be barking.' That's interesting. I wonder why all of us sometimes say some things differently from the way other people say the same things?"

The next step is for the teacher to transcribe the same sentence both ways—the way Jim says it and the way Jenny says it. Nothing should be said about right or wrong because, linguistically speaking, no such value

68

judgments can be made. The differences should be viewed simply as the phenomena they are. We all, in some ways, speak differently, just as we all dress differently, which is one of the things that makes the world interesting.

In time, all the students in a class should come to have some understanding of each other's dialects and, if they have learned well, should be able to switch dialects when it is appropriate to do so. Certainly it is advantageous for a speaker of Black English, let us say, to be able to use the so-called Standard dialect easily.

Teachers must learn to differentiate, however, among the skills they are trying to teach. If, at a given point, their aim is to teach nonreaders to read and to express themselves orally, it might be counterproductive to add to that burden the additional one of learning a new dialect. Learning to read is a complicated process for many students, especially for those from backgrounds that are not notably verbal. To add to this process the additional demands of learning a new dialect—along with trying to figure out what is wrong with the one they have been using and that their loved ones use—might, in some cases, thwart the whole learning process.

WHO SHOULD TRANSCRIBE STUDENT STORIES?

In the early stages of LEA, teachers and aides must necessarily do the writing. In some cases, aides can be drawn from upper elementary classes, and students serving in this capacity will likely improve their own reading and writing skills from such an activity. Aides will need to be trained so that they will know what to write down, how to select from what a student says in order to arrive at a manageable story. However, such training is not complicated and the classroom teacher can provide it quickly.

As time progresses, some students will be able to write their own stories, and, in time, these students can serve as scribes for their LEA groups. Teachers should assist in this process when students, for instance, ask for help in spelling a word. All such student efforts should be displayed in the classroom as prominently as possible.

Some children learn to write before they learn to read or as they are learning to read. Research indicates that early writers are usually better readers than students who begin to write late (14), so it is wise for teachers to offer young students every opportunity to write while they are learning to read. Such prewriting activities as coloring and drawing will often help students develop the small muscle coordination they will require for writing.

Parents can play an important role in helping their children learn to read, and teachers should try to recruit as many parents as they can to serve as aides, if only for an hour a week. Parents who serve as scribes will begin to develop a sense of what the school is doing in reading instruction and probably will find ways of introducing LEA at home. If they have younger children, these children will probably get a head start in learning to read because of their parents' involvement in a primary school reading program (15).

TEACHING CLASSIFICATION THROUGH LEA

One somewhat sophisticated skill that children should be encouraged to learn is classification. This skill, once developed, will serve them well through the rest of their lives, and LEA experience charts can provide an early basis for developing the skill.

Teachers will quickly learn the topics that interest their students. Drawing topics from classroom talk, the teacher should begin with some major categories and should then encourage students to subdivide these major categories as a preparation for story telling. A typical generalized topic that can be subdivided quite productively is the following:

PETS

Pets with Fur	Pets that Swim	Pets that Hop	Pets that Fly
DOGS	GOLDFISH	BUNNIES	CANARIES
CATS	GUPPIES	FROGS	PARAKEETS
BUNNIES	TURTLES	TOADS	FIREFLIES

Every student can contribute to such a chart, and from it productive discussions can ensue. Every student in a typical class will have had experience with at least one of the pets listed, and their stories should provide good material for LEA. The categories should come from the students in the class, not from the teacher. If students are slow to respond, the teacher might prompt them with a well-guided question, such as, "Who can tell us something that some pets do?" or, "Who can tell us what some pets have?" After the first contribution, there should be no dearth of contributions from the rest of the class.

At a slightly higher instructional level, students might see how many pets they can find that fit into more than one category, such as "Bunnies" on the list above. Developing the skill of classification early will help students to organize information as they progress.

MICROCOMPUTERS AND LEA

With the advent of relatively inexpensive microcomputers, the Language Experience Approach has available to it a new dimension. Now teachers can record stories much more quickly than they previously could, and many students are enticed into writing on their own much earlier than was formerly the case. With the microcomputer, it is easy to make multiple copies of stories so that students will be able to keep copies of all the stories written in class. Class books, covered with construction paper and illustrated by students, can provide collections of student stories that can be taken home and read with the guidance of parents. Producing stories in this way should not preclude using hand-printed stories that are transcribed on large sheets of paper and displayed in the classroom; rather it should serve as another means by which stories can be communicated from student to student.

Mark Grabe and Cindy Grabe find that "children gain firsthand experience with writing/reading relationships by learning to read stories they have written. They can extend these insights by learning to read stories dictated by friends" (16). They also find that by involving their students in using interactive stories, which are discussed in some detail in the preceding chapter, students learn a great deal about story structure (17), the knowledge of which has a profound effect upon students' reading skills, especially that of comprehension (18).

Once children begin to compose their stories on microcomputers, they will start to learn about revision, perhaps the most important skill in writing—and one that has been looked upon as arduous until the microcomputer took most of the drudgery out of it. One researcher finds that "using computers may result in longer language experience stories and more revision" (19). Surely the easy erasability of anything that has been written on the microcomputer makes students more likely to take risks in their writing and to experiment with various formats and arrangements of words than was practical when they were working with pencils and paper. Never until now have students had a greater impetus to use written language inventively. With the microcomputer, writing is becoming almost as easy as talking.

Using a number of readily available computer programs, students can make pictures on the computer, and these pictures can serve as a basis for student stories. Teachers can gain valuable insights into individual student perceptions by making copies of a picture and having each student in a group write or tell a story relating to the picture. Roy A. Moxley and Pamela A. Barry suggest that useful programs that allow students to compose pictures are *Faspictures—Letters, Faspictures—Words,* and *Faspicturewriting* (20).

LEA AS A GATEWAY TO READING

The Language Experience Approach is a gateway to reading in two essential ways. In the first place, it encourages students to read their own stories and, as they progress, stories their classmates and friends have told. They approach these stories with a feeling of involvement, excitement, and pride. Secondly, teachers will quickly come to know what their students' interests and enthusiams are through listening to their stories, and this will enable them to work toward broadening their students' perspectives by reading or telling them stories that reflect their interests and by leading them to stories, perhaps in basal readers, that will probably appeal to them.

It has been shown that students increase their reading comprehension when they learn to see inferences in stories, when they develop their ability to predict what is likely to happen (21). Interactive stories can help move students in this direction, and teachers can also encourge students to guess outcomes in the stories they read or tell to them. When student stories are preserved on diskettes, teachers can also edit them into cloze procedure exercises, leaving out substantive words that students reading the stories will supply.

HUMOR IN THE READING CLASSROOM

The more people know about the workings and possibilities of language, the more likely they are to use it in humorous ways, particularly for punning. Working with puns and riddles can help young students learn more about language in a way that is appealing to them. Eleanore S. Tyson and Lee Mountain show how riddles can "provide two ingredients that are important for vocabulary learning: context clues and high-interest materials" (22). Riddles lead into puns, as these writers point out. They classify riddles in relation to the type of humor they involve: homonyms, rhyming words, double meaning, figurative/literal meaning, and intonation (23).

Understanding humor in each of these classifications leads students to a more sophisticated understanding of language. Even prereaders can begin work with homonyms, rhyming words, and intonation. As these students mature as readers, but often while they are still in the first or second grades, they will be capable of dealing with double meanings and with the differences between literal and figurative meaning.

In dealing with the latter, for example, teachers might have students illustrate the literal meaning of figurative statements: "She eats like a bird" or "He works like a horse" or "He's as fast as a speeding bullet" or "It is raining cats and dogs." Students can have great fun, also, dreaming up rhyming answers to questions: What is beautiful New York? (A pretty city) What is a laughing half dollar? (Funny money) What is a mean hammer? (Cruel tool) What is a dishwasher? (A clean machine).

Jokes and riddles are particularly good vehicles for presenting cloze exercises. In fact, initial work in the cloze procedure will probably go easily if the procedure is used in connection with homonyms or in riddles.

SURROUNDING STUDENTS WITH PRINTED MATERIALS

Students enter school with varying bases of experience. Those whose bases of experience are quite limited begin school with a handicap. Teachers cannot provide such students with what they have been deprived of in their earliest years, but they can do everything in their power to understand their deficits and to help them catch up.

Sheila Bernal Guzmán, who teaches students from a low socioeconomic area of Austin, Texas, approaches these students, many of whom would predictably fall behind in reading, with energy and understanding. She has found ways to emphasize print in her kindergarten class, and typically *all* of her students are able to read after a year in her classroom. The special magic in Guzmán's teaching is in part attributable to the fact that she came from the same background as many of her Mexican-American students and that she realizes from her own background "that children from lower socioeconomic level homes often have limited experiences with written materials. Books are not the common objects for them that they are for most middle and upper-class children" (24).

Guzmán begins to involve her kindergarten students with print on their first day in her class. She prints each student's name in colorful block letters on name tags, and has them wear these tags. She makes sure that they recognize their own names and also encourages them to recognize the names of their classmates so that they can help to pass out papers and workbooks in class.

Guzmán makes sure that students in her class see their names frequently on papers and on other materials. She also labels objects and places in the room in both English and Spanish so that children become familiar with print as a means of identifying things. As children begin to read the name tags of other children, and as they begin to be able to read the signs around the room, Guzman puts them into reading groups. She also works individually with each student in three- to five-minute intervals, asking them whether they can read. Most say they cannot, but she reminds them that they can read their names. She then asks them what other words they would like to learn to read, and she prints these words on separate cards, giving them a set to use in school and another set to take home.

As students move toward reading an increasing number of words, they are encouraged to write stories and to make these stories into books that they can share with their friends and take home to show their parents. By moving her students more and more into the use of print, with which they are surrounded in her classroom, Guzmán achieves remarkable results with students whose chances of performing at an above average reading level were initially slim.

By understanding what their students need and what their backgrounds have failed to provide them with before they enter school, all teachers of young children can help these children make incredible strides toward learning to read effectively and toward enjoying reading as a means of finding out things they want to know. The Language Experience Approach offers the best hope for students at this level as long as it is combined with work in phonic analysis and, in some cases, with at least a limited use of basal readers.

Chapter 7
PHONICS AND READING INSTRUCTION

PHONICS DEFINED

Phonics allows readers to recognize the relationship between a sound and its written form, usually between a single letter (*b, d, t,* etc.) or a combination of letters (blends such as *bl* and *tr*; digraphs such as *ch* and *sh*; and diphthongs such as *oi, ou* as in *out*, and *ow* as in *now*) and the corresponding sound that such letters represent. Letters do not have sounds as such; they merely are a means by which commonly agreed upon graphemes represent their corresponding phonemes. People who understand these correspondences can read most words—even words they have never encountered before—with a fair degree of accuracy.

As you look at this page, you can sound out the letters of *renafutopid* even though you have never seen it before and even though it is not a word in the English language (nor likely in any other language). You may not know where to accent such a word, but you can pronounce it. Having sounded it out, it will have no meaning for you because you have never before encountered it and it is not presented in any context. If, however, you sound out *baseball*, assuming that you have never before seen that word, you will probably make the association between the letters on the page in that specific combination and a word that is part of your oral vocabulary. From that standpoint, a knowledge and understanding of phonics can be a boon to beginning readers. Endless numbers of words can be sounded out if one possesses even a limited knowledge of phonics.

WHAT LETTERS ARE MOST IMPORTANT?

Teachers do not teach phonics by working their way through the alphabet from *a* to *z*. Some letters are more efficiently and productively taught to beginning readers than others. Teachers must decide early whether to teach consonants or vowels first or whether to teach them in combination. They need to decide whether to place emphasis on whole words or on parts of words, such as the initial sound and its graphemic representation. They must determine the order in which letters will be taught.

Usually consonants are taught before vowels. Consonants correspond more nearly to their sounds than vowels do. Paul McKee believes that a knowledge of those commonly occurring consonants that usually represent just one sound in English (*b*, *d*, *f*, *h*, *j*, *k*, *l*, *m*, *n*, *p*, *r*, *t*, *v*, and *w*) will enable students to read some basic materials (1). They will be able to do some contextual guessing and will supply vowel sounds even though they might not know their vowels by sight at this point. Such students would certainly be able to make a more successful attempt at reading *Jan had Dan to her den* without knowing vowels (J–n h–d D–n t– h–r d–n) than without knowing consonants (–a– –a– –a– –o –e– –e–), but they would predictably make some miscues in reading the sentence if it were rendered with all of its vowels missing. Nevertheless, the sound of each consonant gives a significant clue to what appears on the page.

The *order of primitivity*, developed by the Institute of Logopedics at the University of Wichita, is based upon physiological data that indicate that consonantal sounds originally developed in language in the following order: *m*, *p*, *b*, *t*, *d*, *n*, *h*, *w*, *f*, *v*, *k*, *g*, *th*, *sh*, *zh*, *ch*, *j*, *s*, *z*, *r*, and *l* (2). Emerald Dechant states: "Experience shows that when a child suffers speech loss, the loss is in reverse order. The last sounds to be developed are the first sounds to be lost" (3), and most students tend to develop sounds in this order.

Clearly, the letters that should be taught first are those that have the most regular correspondences to the sound they represent. From this group, the most frequently used letters should be taught first. Letters whose names do not correspond to their sounds (notably *h* and *w*) should not be taught until children have developed a secure grounding in basic phonics. Letters that occur infrequently, particularly those that represent more than one sound, should not be used or taught in the earliest stages of reading instruction. Among these are *x*, which can represent six different sounds, but which most often represents one of two sounds—*ks* or *gz*; *q*, which in English cannot be used in isolation and which is pronounced *kw* with the addition of *u*; *k*, which is fairly infrequent and is identical in sound to the *c* in *cat*; *v*, which is infrequent and will confuse children from Spanish-speaking backgrounds; *y*, which sometimes has almost a consonantal value, as in *yes* and other initial positions, but is a vowel in 97 percent of its occurrences, as in *day* (4); and *z*, which is infrequently used and has different sounds in, for example, *zebra* and *azure* (5).

WHAT DOES EARLY READING INSTRUCTION DEMAND?

Assuming that a child in the early stages of learning to read has already mastered the left-right, top-to-bottom directional conventions of reading English texts, the decoding process is one of the most complex challenges imposed upon anyone in any learning situation. A study by Betty Berdiansky and others (6) has analyzed 6,092 one- and two-syllable words drawn from over 9,000 different words they culled from the speaking and writing of a large number of children in the six-to-nine age group. Analyzing these words, they found that children, in order to learn to decode them, would have to have been exposed to 211 distinct and discrete phoneme-grapheme correspondences. They would have to have encountered situations relating to 166 rules, 60 of which relate to consonants specifically, and 69 of which are spelling pattern rules. Of the 166 basic rules, 45 would have exceptions.

Part of the reason for such complications stems from the fact that English has a borrowed alphabet, the Roman alphabet, which is suited to the phonology of the Latin language. In English, between 39 and 44 sounds (depending on which linguist you read) must be represented with a basic alphabet of 26 letters. This means that some letters must represent more than one sound (like the *c* in *can* and *ceiling* or the *s* in *same* and *his*) and that certain combinations of letters are used to create other sounds (as *ph* /f/ or *sh* /sh/, each of which is a single sound even though it is graphemically represented by two letters).

Some letters that have come to us from the Romans have no phonemes of their own in English (*c*, aforementioned; *x*, which can represent any of six different sounds; and *q*, which cannot be used alone and which in combination with *u* produces the blend /k/ /w/ and in combination with *ue* is rendered /k/ as in *queue* or *unique* or *plaque*). Some letters are silent—for example, the *k* in *know*, the *w* in *whole*, the *c* in *track*, and the *gh* in *daughter*. Terminal *e* is generally silent in English, although it will alter the sound value of the preceding vowel, which is what differentiates *mat* from *mate* and *rot* from *rote*. But this rule is not consistent: *for* and *fore* are pronounced exactly alike.

Vowels are more difficult to teach than consonants because they have less sound-letter relationship than consonants. The only vowel that represents only a vowel sound is *a*. For every other vowel there are exceptional usages that relate to a consonant sound: *e* in *azalea* is consonantal /y/; *u* is both consonantal /y/ (*unite*) and /w/ (*persuade*); *o* is /w/ in *choir* and *one* (7). The terminal /e/ sound in English is usually rendered by *y*:

many, *happily*, etc. Although experienced readers deal easily and naturally with these and a host of other problem words—particularly with such homonyms as *cite/site/sight*, *one/won*, *for/fore/four*, *ceil/seal*, *sail/sale*, and *choir/quire*, and hundreds of other similarly confusing words—beginning readers who try to sound out such words phonically may have incredible difficulty. Teachers need to be sufficiently sensitive to their students' dialects to know whether such pairs as *talk/tock* and *daughter/dotter* are homonyms for them, as they frequently are in some dialects of English.

UNDERSTANDING THE FINAL E

Probably before they do any formal work specifically with long vowel sounds and with the corresponding letters, students need to know that a final *e* preceded by a consonant that is preceded by a vowel usually lengthens the sound of the preceding vowel so that, as we have noted, *fat* becomes *fate* and *rot* becomes *rote*. This is a fairly consistent rule, but it is not always operative; if it were, *come* and *comb* would have the same pronunciation. However, in *come* and *done* the *o*, rather than being sounded as a long *o*, is sounded as a short *u*.

In an early phonics approach, which is a letter-by-letter approach or, in oral reading, a sound-by-sound approach, beginning readers process a word by proceeding from left to right, sounding each letter as they go, until they produce a familiar set of consecutive sounds and know that they have read a word. The order of their reading in a word like *FAT* is a 1–2–3 order, at the end of which the word *fat* has been sounded out. However, if they are dealing with the very similarly spelled word *FATE*, they find themselves forced, if they are to read correctly, to follow a new pattern of word attack: 1–2–3–4–2–3 or 1–2–3–4–3–2.

The number of eye movements involved is now six rather than the three involved with *fat*. But over and above this, a new reading protocol must be advanced so that they understand what the introduction of the final *e* rule demands of them. Teachers need to appreciate the complexity of this process which, for most of them, is simple and automatic.

TEACHING VOWELS

Because vowel sounds are less uniform in their phonemic-graphemic correspondences than consonant sounds, they present special learning problems for beginning readers. Regional differences are more noticeable in vowel sounds than in consonant sounds. In some parts of the country, *tan*, *ten*, and *tin* are virtually indistinguishable from each other. Whereas Albert J. Mazurkiewicz distinguishes 168 consonant graphemes (as opposed to the approximately 18 consonants found in the Roman alphabet), he identifies 265 vowel graphemes that represent a total of 16 vowel phonemes (8). Given this complicated situation, teachers should first help their students to differentiate between short and long vowels.

Because short vowels are more frequent in English than long vowels are, they should be taught first. If students guess at the vowel sound in word attack, they are more likely to guess correctly if they give the vowel the short sound. The sound values of short vowels are as follows:

> *a* as in *bat, attire, about*
>
> *e* as in *bend, elm, help*
>
> *i* as in *bin, inch, improve*
>
> *o* as in *bottle, dot, rob*
>
> *u* as in *uncle, study, but*

Read in isolation, long vowels are sounded like vowel letters in the alphabet, even though the graphemic representation may be a digraph. That is, the *ee* in *bee* and the *ea* in *sea* are pronounced identically and sound just like the letter *e* would sound if someone were reciting the alphabet. The long *a* sound may have many graphemic representations (*ai* as in *sail*, *ay* as in *pay*, *et* as in *filet*, *er* as in *dossier*, *aigh* as in *straight*, etc.); yet it is always pronounced just as the first letter of the alphabet is pronounced by someone saying the ABCs.

Students should also be introduced ultimately to the open syllable rule: when a syllable ends in a vowel sound, the vowel is long, as in *hu-mid*, or *re-cent*. When a syllable ends in a consonant sound, the vowel is short, as in *con-sent*. This rule cannot be taught before students have worked on syllabification. It is a useful rule to know, however, and it should be taught, despite its notable exceptions.

SPELLING IRREGULARITIES

In early reading instruction, as we will note in the following chapter on linguistics and the teaching of reading, it is probably best not to expose beginning readers to most irregularly spelled words until they have gained considerable ability and confidence in reading regularly spelled words. Leonard Bloomfield adhered to this principle to the extent that he excluded from his earliest lessons such words as *the*, *mother*, and *father*, which somewhat limited the range of sentences he could make. Perhaps some exceptions should be made, as they were in Fries's program, but the number of exceptions should be limited stringently.

Jack Bagford suggests, "High frequency, but irregularly sounded, words probably are more efficiently taught by a sight method while phonetically regular words and words which contain easily learned sounds probably are better taught by a phonic method" (9). Bagford calls for an eclectic approach to early reading instruction and is moderate in his tone, reminding teachers, "Phonics content is taught so that children have a tool to identify words which are known in the spoken form but not in the printed form" (10). By combining phonics and the sight word approach, beginning students can enjoy the best of two possible worlds, and early reading materials can be more varied and better related to student interest than would be possible if the phonics approach were used exclusively.

ATTEMPTS TO REFORM SPELLING

The inadequacy of the Roman alphabet to represent fully and directly the sounds of English—which is a Germanic, not a Romance language—has caused all sorts of inventive people including Benjamin Franklin (11) to suggest ways of reforming English spelling (12). Dennis E. Baron reports that in 1906, President Theodore Roosevelt issued an order demanding simplified spelling, but nothing ever came of this order because our spelling conventions, as illogical as they are, appear to be essentially too ingrained in the populace to be changed (13). In the 1930s, however, the *Chicago Tribune* did adopt reformed spelling and for years published its paper in accordance with its new spelling rules, which rendered *through* as *thru*, *night* as *nite*, etc. (14)

Relatively few such reforms reached the schools in any organized way, although in the late 1960s and early 1970s Sir James Pitman, a Briton, devised what was first called an "Augmented Roman Alphabet." This developed into what is commonly referred to as the "Initial Teaching Alphabet," often rendered merely i. t. a.

Pitman, the grandson of Sir Isaac Pitman who in 1837 devised a means of transcription that grew into the Pitman method of shorthand, proposed that i. t. a. be used only for initial reading instruction and writes that "as soon as fluency in reading with the new alphabet has been achieved, the transition is made to reading with the orthodox roman alphabet" (15).

In Pitman's scheme, every long vowel has its own symbol so that readers are guided to precisely the intended pronunciation. The terminal *s* in a word like *was* is rendered with a backward *z* (ζ): the word *was* would be written *woζ*. Words like *said* and *dead* would be written *sed* and *ded*, respectively. One who can read conventional English can read a text written in Pitman's system with no special training. This variation on the Roman alphabet might have yielded encouraging results; however, the system was tested extensively, and the preponderance of research data available indicates that while exposure to the system appears not to have harmed beginning readers, it did not improve their performance. Most schools have now abandoned the use of i. t. a.

THE ANALYTICAL AND SYNTHETIC APPROACHES

Phonics can be taught analytically or synthetically. The analytical approach begins with the whole word and then breaks it down (analyzes it) into its component phonic elements. The synthetic approach begins with the graphemic-phonemic correspondences that students first learn and then apply by blending the sounds of the letters in words into consecutive utterances that result in a pronounceable unit (a word, unless students are dealing with nonsense syllables). Although the analytical approach is more popular among teachers (16), research evidence suggests that it is less effective than the synthetic approach.

In a study conducted in Virginia, data were collected and compared for 484 first grade students; 248 were taught according to the analytical approach and 236 according to the synthetic approach. The groups were essentially equal in age, ability, and background. The researchers report that "When the means of the synthetic program groups ... are compared with those of the analytical program groups, ... a great preponderance of differences among means (92 out of 125, or 75 percent) is found to be significantly in favor of the synthetic group. In only three instances are the obtained differences in favor of the analytical group" (17). This is compelling research evidence in favor of the synthetic approach, and it supports some important conclusions Jeanne Chall reached in *Learning to Read: The Great Debate*: "A recent study by Bleismer and Yarborough (1965), published after a major portion of this chapter was written, tends to confirm my basic interpretations of the past classroom experiments as well as my judgment that a novelty [Hawthorne] effect did not have a major influence on their results" (18).

CHALL's *LEARNING TO READ: THE GREAT DEBATE*

Perhaps the most valuable book to date that deals extensively with the subject of phonics is Chall's *Learning to Read: The Great Debate*, which has examined every significant research study in reading done between 1910 and 1965. Its conclusions and recommendations should not be ignored—although many of them have been.

Chall does not vacillate in her statement of how initial reading should be taught if it is to be most effective: "The evidence from the experimental studies analyzed so far indicates that unselected children taught initially by a code-emphasis generally do better in reading than children taught by a meaning-emphasis, at least up to early fourth grade" (19). More recent researchers have reached quite opposite conclusions. Connie Juel and Diane Roper-Schneider conclude that "while the materials may be influential in influencing early letter-sound correspondence knowledge, sheer exposure to lots of words also allows children to induce this information. Results further suggest that first graders who do indeed acquire such knowledge do better both in reading the words in their basals *and* reading words on which they have not received instruction" (20).

It is evident that much more research needs to be done on phonics and its relationship to reading, both to decoding and to heightening comprehension. Future researchers might also examine the adult reading abilities of people over 20 who were taught by the two methods. Some researchers feel that the whole word approach in the long run produces readers whose speed and comprehension are better than the speed and comprehension of people who learned to read through the synthetic phonics approach. To date no hard evidence suggests that this is the case.

With the caveats that (1) she endorses the code-emphasis approach only for beginning reading and (2) she does not endorse one code-emphasis method over another, Chall writes that "the research from 1912 to 1965 indicates that a code-emphasis method—i.e., one that views beginning reading as essentially different from mature reading and emphasizes learning of the printed code for the spoken language—produces better results, at least up to the point where sufficient evidence seems to be available, the end of the third grade" (21). This statement is cautious, as is most of what Chall says, but it is also unequivocal.

82

The appearance of the Chall book did not mark the conclusion of the great debate; that flourishes still. Major research data are still coming in. More data will be required to answer many of the questions that have been raised; but for the time, it seems clear that the old phonics approach of the New England primer was not completely ineffective.

THE McGUFFEY READERS: DIDACTIC AND ANALYTICAL

The ever-popular *McGuffey Readers*, which stressed meaning and required students to identify and memorize sight words at the beginning of each selection, used what would today be called an analytical phonics approach to some extent. That is, they taught pupils "to identify words and read sentences. . . . Having read a few lessons in this manner," William H. McGuffey tells the teacher, "begin to use the Phonic Method, combining it with the Word Method, by first teaching the words in each lesson as words; then, the elementary sounds, the names of the letters, and spelling" (22). These readers have begun to come back into vogue, largely because of the back-to-the-basics movement, but teachers should be cautioned that no research evidence exists to suggest that this approach yields promising results in beginning students.

Perhaps the didactic approach is the only feasible one to use with children at ages five or six. Mazurkiewicz writes, "Discovery-type decoding instruction, though successful in the case of many pupils, apparently has not been effective in increasing reading achievement in a large number of others since, according to Piagetian theory, the average child has not yet developed sufficient cognitive skills to allow him or her to induce the grapheme-phoneme relationships" (23). This is not to say that the primary school years are not a time of discovery; rather it suggests that in beginning reading instruction, the discovery method is inefficient. In a typical school day, the opportunity for discovery is great and skill in reading can help to promote it. But the students need to gain skill in reading at this stage of development, and the great weight of reliable research evidence cited by Chall and Mazurkiewicz, both of whom have been exhaustive in their investigations, indicates categorically that the didactic method of beginning reading instruction will lead students most effectively to the desired ends.

Recent research findings by Barbara Nemko reveal that among two groups of first grade students in two inner-city elementary schools, students who learned words in isolation and by rote had better word recognition after 24 hours than did students who learned words in contextual situations (24), a finding that seems to support those of Chall and Mazurkiewicz.

A FINAL WORD

Teachers of reading, particularly those involved in initial reading instruction, need to believe in what they are doing, and they must approach their task with a solid base of research information to support them in the procedures they use. Some eclecticism is healthy and desirable; not all children learn best by the same method. However, teachers must be aware of the research data that are continually coming in if they are to be informed professionals who can work with young children to help them to gain possession of the skill the modern world values above all others—literacy.

Chapter 8
LINGUISTICS AND
READING INSTRUCTION

WHAT IS LINGUISTICS?

The term *linguistics* can be defined in various ways. The general term is used to include such areas as *historical linguistics*, which has to do with the historical development of language through the ages; *descriptive linguistics*, which is concerned with both speech sounds (phonology) and grammar (how language patterns are structured, which in turn involves morphology and syntax); *linguistic geography* and *dialectology*, both of which catalog and describe languages as they are used in various regions by various groups of people; and *comparative linguistics*, which is concerned with relationships among various languages of common origin, such as the Indo-European family of languages or, more narrowly, the Romance or Germanic languages, both of which are subdivisions of the Indo-European group. Overlaps exist within these classifications. Comparative linguistics, for example, is much concerned with the historical development of languages and with linguistic geography.

Charles C. Fries states: "Most 'linguists' study languages in order to know and to understand their structures—the particular ways in which these languages use their linguistic units to achieve their communicative function. They seek, primarily, knowledge about the units and the working processes of each language rather than the ability to speak them" (1). Most linguists are fundamentally concerned with studying the spoken language and view it as the quintessential and most revealing form of language; writing is a relatively new invention when compared to the length of time that language has been used in some systematic way for the purpose of communication. Although most current linguists are concerned with language in all aspects of its use, the sounds of language—both as perceived by listeners and, more importantly, as physiologically produced by speakers—are of extraordinary concern to them.

Frank Smith points to some of the limits that surround the field of linguistics: "Linguists in general are concerned with the abstract study of language—they analyze and compare such aspects of languages as their sounds, syntax, and lexicon; they examine similarities and differences among languages, and try to trace their evolutionary development. Linguists are concerned with the nature of language as a system that is available to its users, rather than with the way in which language is acquired, produced, and comprehended by individuals'' (2).

Modern linguistics has gathered and organized its information about language according to scientific principles. Modern grammarians (linguists) are concerned with how language operates. They generally do not acknowledge correctness or incorrectness in language; language either communicates or does not communicate. In studying groups that use a given language or dialect, most linguists have concluded that, regardless of the social status of the language or dialect in question, it is sufficient to meet the communication needs of its users. Within its own context it is effective and appropriate.

LINGUISTIC TERMINOLOGY

As linguistic influences have been felt in the teaching of reading, reading teachers have had to equip themselves with some of the terminology of linguists in order to understand what linguistically-oriented systems are conveying. The following minimal vocabulary of 20 terms will be useful to teachers:

allophone: A variant or subclass of a phoneme. For example, the *p* in *put* and the *p* in *spire* are allophones; the former is aspirated, the latter unaspirated.

alphabet: A set of written symbols that represent the sounds of a language.

alphabetic writing: Writing in which graphemes are used to represent the sounds of a language; a highly abstract form of writing.

code: The representation of the written language.

decode: To identify written letters or words by making graphemic-phonemic correspondences.

dialect: A variant form of a root language, usually spoken by members of a given group or social class, or by residents of a particular geographic area, such as the language of the aristocracy, Boston English, British English, ghettoese, and Pidgin English.

digraph: A pair of letters representing a single speech sound, as in m*ea*t, s*ee*m, gra*ph*, *pn*eumonia, and *kn*ig*h*t.

diphthong: A blend of a vowel sound with a near-vowel sound, as in *ai*l, *ou*r, pl*oy*, and *ou*nce; sometimes a diphthong is represented by a single letter, as in *a*le, *u*se, or *i*sle.

grapheme: The written representation of a sound; each letter of the alphabet is a grapheme; pictographs and ideographs may also be designated as graphemes.

graphemic-phonemic correspondence: The relationship that exists between graphemes and their corresponding sounds.

ideographic writing: Writing in which a visual symbol represents an idea although nothing about its shape or form as such suggests that idea; the concept *house* may be represented by a symbol that does not look like a house, and the concept *man* may be represented by a symbol that does not look like a man.

method of contrast: A means of identifying specific phonemes by the comparison and contrast of minimal pairs.

minimal pairs: Pairs of words that sound the same except for one phoneme: *day* and *ray*, *tower* and *power*, *fall* and *ball*, *fan* and *far*.

morpheme: A linguistic unit that carries meaning and contains no smaller meaningful parts, such as *sun*, *day*, *pry*, or *port* (free forms) or port*s*, *re*port, sunn*ed*, pry*ing*, da*i*ly (bound forms because they are dependent upon other forms for their meanings).

phoneme: The smallest unit of speech in any language that distinguishes one utterance from another; *p* distinguishes *pan* from *fan* or from *ban*; *w* distinquishes *west* from *rest* or from *best*.

phonemics: The study of the sounds (phonemes) in a language that are significant in that they differentiate words that are the same except for one sound: *pet* and *met*, *pet* and *pen*, *hoot* and *loot*, *loot* and *loom*.

phonetics: The study of speech sounds as elements of language as they are conceived physiologically and perceived auditorially.

phonics: The study of sound, particularly of graphemic-phonemic relationships that are stressed in some methods of initial reading instruction; phonics in its early stages may stress the sounding of individual letters out of context; some phonics systems begin with the whole word rather than with the parts that constitute it.

pictographic writing: The oldest form of writing, in which the graphic form looks like the concept it is intended to represent; the pictograph for *house* would resemble a house and that for *man* would resemble a man.

syntax: The way morphemes are put together into comprehensible patterns.

SPELLING AS A LINGUISTIC ACTIVITY

Teachers can learn a great deal about the linguistic sophistication of young students by understanding how and why they spell as they do. Just as miscue analysis can provide teachers with valuable clues about the mental processes of students as they read aloud, so can an analysis of spelling errors provide insights about the level of linguistic development a student is displaying.

J. Richard Gentry identifies four levels of development in early readers: prephonemic spelling, early phonemic spelling, letter name spelling, and transitional spelling (3). At the first stage, children simply draw random letters, perhaps in a series, but they produce nothing that has meaning. In the second stage, children are beginning to realize that letters represent sounds and might render a word like *book* as *bkk* or a word like *fish* as *fss* (4).

As they approach reading readiness, children will begin to move toward letter name spelling. They will probably not represent silent letters at this point, nor will all of their letters be correct, but they are beginning to show increased knowledge of sound-letter relationships, and they know from which parts of the mouth various sounds come. For example, they may spell *truck* as *churk* because they know that the *tr* sound comes form the same region of the mouth as the *ch* sound, after which they have to insert a vowel if the word is to be pronounced, so the *r* is metathesized (5).

As students move to the transitional stage, they begin to be more aware of word structures and of the effect of silent letters on pronunciation. They might misspell *bite* as *biet* or *byt* because they are aware that the *i* in it is different from the *i* in *bit*. Actually, such a misspelling indicates that the student is beginning to internalize spelling information and that this might be a good time to teach him or her about the silent E rule.

LINGUISTIC INFLUENCES ON READING INSTRUCTION

Linguistic science did not exert significant influence on reading instruction in any organized way until the 1960s, although Bloomfield's work in the field began as early as 1937 (6) and Fries's initial interest in the linguistic implications of reading instruction predated 1960, despite the fact that his *Linguistics and Reading* was not completed until 1962.

By 1960, structural linguistics, a subfield of descriptive linguistics, had received considerable attention from language teachers at all levels; Noam Chomsky had published his historic *Syntactic Structures* three years earlier, and the new transformational-generative grammar that he introduced was beginning to intrigue people interested in language learning. Modern scientific theories about language were proliferating, and concentrated attention was soon to be focused on reading instruction—by the linguists and, yet more intensely, by those who, although not linguists themselves, found the linguists' work with language promising and exciting.

From descriptive linguists like Bloomfield and Fries were to come reassessments of how people learn to decode written language (graphemic representation) and either translate the graphemes into the sounds of language orally or comprehend the graphemes in some meaningful way—that is, get sense out of what they are reading. Dolores Durkin calls decoding "the process of identifying written words on the basis of *grapheme-phoneme correspondences*" (7). Bloomfield and Fries both developed systems for the initial teaching of reading (decoding).

During the same period, linguistic geographers and comparative linguists were turning serious attention to the study of dialects. Hans Kurath had made phenomenal progress in cataloging regional differences in American English in the *Linguistic Atlas of the United States and Canada*, which he edited until his work was taken over by Raven McDavid, Jr., who served as senior editor of the *Atlas* until his death in

1984. This pioneering work paved the way for sociolinguists, who began to study dialects scientifically and who demonstrated convincingly that all dialects are reasonably regular in their morphology and syntax and that some dialect usages are more regular (*I was*, *you was*, *he was*, for example) or more logical (I have three brother) (8) than comparable constructions in so-called Standard English.

The sociolinguists did much to disabuse language arts teachers of the notion that one dialect is more correct than another; rather they suggested that one dialect is appropriate for some situations and another appropriate for other situations, just as jeans are fine for a hayride and more formal attire is sensible for a job interview with the vice-president of a bank. Linguists of every bent have proclaimed that language is constantly changing (which is why average speakers of English today cannot read *Beowulf* in the original without special instruction) and have rejoiced in the fact.

They also have pointed out that while some elements of language change, others lag behind; hence, we say *nite* but usually write *night*, we say *enuff* but usually write *enough*, we say *dauter* (in some dialects *dotter*) but usually write *daughter*. Each of these words was once pronounced as it is still recorded graphemically. The phonology has now changed, but the graphology has in most cases not reflected the change. Many common words are now obviously in the process of change. *Strength*, with its two bewildering clusters of consonants, is very difficult for most people to pronounce, so while *strength* is still heard, *strenth* and *strent* are not uncommon pronunciations as well. What Charlton Laird wrote in 1953 has been amply supported by the sociolinguists of the 1960s and 1970s: "Speakers of a language take it as they use it, and do not think much about its past or future. They think of it as 'right' or 'wrong,' but they are not much aware that the *wrongs* may become *rights* and the *rights* become *obsoletes*" (9).

While descriptive linguists and sociolinguists were unraveling some of the puzzles and perplexities of how language operates, psycholinguists were exploring some of the psychological phenomena of how people use language and of what we can glean about the language-learning process from the clues provided by normal language use. Among the fruitful investigations motivated by psycholinguistics, perhaps none is quite so important and revealing as miscue analysis.

The remainder of this chapter deals with the notable contributions of Bloomfield and Fries to reading instruction. Subsequent chapters deal separately with the influential areas of miscue analysis and dialectology.

BLOOMFIELD's SYSTEM

Leonard Bloomfield's interest in reading instruction was an outgrowth of his experience in helping his own son learn to read. Approaching this problem as a linguistic scientist, he naturally applied the linguistic conventions in which he had been well schooled to the new field in which he sought to achieve a degree of mastery.

Bloomfield begins with the assumption that it is not possible to understand reading without also understanding "the relation of written (or printed) words to speech" (10). He feels that reading can be effectively taught in a much shorter period than is usually required to teach it.

Bloomfield points out the relative newness of reading and writing in comparison to the whole span of human existence and also notes that, even today, more languages exist solely in oral form than exist in written form. He calls writing artificial in comparison to speaking. He differentiates among picture writing (pictographic writing), word writing (ideographic writing), and alphabetic writing, noting that the last is capable of nuances and specificities of which the other two forms of writing are not. He notes that once people know the sounds of their language as these sounds are graphemically recorded, they can sound out, with a high degree of uniformity, words of which they do not know the meanings. This is not true of the ideographs that linger in our language—*10* means *ten*; but whereas readers can sound out *t-e-n*, there is nothing in *10* to tell them how it is pronounced. The *1* in *10* does not represent a sound. If it did, *11*, *12*, *13*, etc., would all have the same initial sound. Such signs as *$*, *#*, *&*, and *½* and such abbreviations as *Ave.*, *Mr.*, *Apt.*, *Assn.*, and *etc.* also give readers few clues to the actual pronunciation of the words they represent.

Bloomfield contends with disarming simplicity, "In order to understand the nature of alphabetic writing we need know only what is meant by the term *unit speech sound*, or, as the linguist calls it, by the term *phoneme*" (11). All human utterances are combinations of phonemes. For those who know the language being spoken, the combinations sound intelligible; for those who do not know the language, the phonemes are meaningless noise. Phonemes in English have graphemic representations. The 26 letters of our alphabet, alone or in combination, yield approximately 42 sounds of which all English words are composed in one way or another. The sound-letter relationship in English is said to be only about 20 percent efficient (12), so it is perhaps not surprising that some students have difficulty learning to read.

Bloomfield removes from the paths of students some of the initial obstacles that the somewhat inefficient sound-letter relationship in English imposes. He starts students with regular words, enabling them to develop strategies for figuring out language before exposing them to irregular words like *was, one, knee, gnu,* or *Phil.* Bloomfield demands that students work systematically with words, beginning with sets or groups of similar two- or three-letter words that differ in only one phoneme: *at, bat, cat, fat, gat, hat, lat, mat, rat*—but never *eat* which totally confuses the issue—or *bud, bug, bum, bun, bus, but.* Bloomfield has no objection to allowing students to pronounce words that are not commonly in the language—for example, *lat* in the list above—because in so doing they reinforce their ability to make grapheme-phoneme correspondences and also because they will later encounter some of the nonsense syllables in other contexts, such as *lattice* or *lateral.*

Initially Bloomfield introduces students to all the vowels but to only one pronunciation of each vowel: *a* as in *cat; e* as in *pet; i* as in *pin; o* as in *hot;* and *u* as in *cut.* He introduces all the consonants except *q* and *x,* but he introduces them in words in which they have the same sound: if *get,* then not *gem;* if *cut,* then not *cent.*

He notes that the list of consonants contains one duplication—*c* as in *cat* and *k* are the same phoneme; he contends that this will not cause a reading difficulty, although it may cause a spelling difficulty when the student writes. Essentially, the first thing Bloomfield is aiming for is consistency. The English language is inconsistent, but Bloomfield isolates consistent elements within it and uses these elements in the early stages of reading instruction, allowing students initially to establish a secure and dependable reading base.

Before children are introduced to groups of words, Bloomfield advocates giving them visual discrimination tests and asking them to read letters of the alphabet, first in capital block letters, then in both upper- and lower-case block letters, sounding out each letter individually.

Part One of Bloomfield's scheme, then, deals exclusively with groups of two- or three-letter words, all quite regular and consistent in their pronunciation. Part Two, while maintaining the regular pronunciations of each letter, presents words with two (and sometimes three) consecutive consonants that students should be able to pronounce by sounding the letters as they have learned to sound them: *spit, split, clip, grip, strip.* Later in Part Two, "regular" values are assigned to some more problematic areas of pronunciation: *-ing* as in *sing; -nk* as in *link; -sh* or *sh-* as in *fish* or *shot; -ch* or *ch-* as in *inch* or *chin; -th* or *th-* as in *fifth* or *thin;*

wh- as in *when*; *-ck* as in *back*; and *-tch* as in *catch*. By the conclusion of Part Two, *is*, *was*, *mother*, *father*, *brother*, *than*, *they*, and *them* have not been introduced because these words contain irregular pronunciations. As has been noted earlier, this limits the content of the reading material, and many teachers have objected that the readings fail to capitalize on the interests of beginning reading students because of the scrupulous omission of irregular sounds. The sentences that Bloomfield and Barnhart have constructed from the words available are no less interesting, however, than those found in more conventional basal readers of the period during which these two linguists were writing. Part Two concludes with the introduction of *x* as in *box* and *qu* as in *quit*. The spelling of each is treated as regular.

Part Three introduces pairs of vowels (*ee*, *ea*, *oo*, etc.) and pairs consisting of a vowel and a semivowel (*ay*, *aw*, *ew*, etc.). It is not until Part Four that irregular formations are introduced, and by this time children have developed a good sense of sound-letter correspondence and should be reading the materials in the first three lessons with relative ease and accuracy. As the program grows increasingly more difficult, students will have been drilled in large quantities of words but should have been only minimally confused by them because of the consistency of sound-letter correspondences within them.

Teachers have had reservations about the Bloomfield materials because they are not accompanied by illustrations; Bloomfield generally preferred not to give students a pictographic crutch to lean on while they were attempting to learn alphabetic versions of words (13). He was explicit in saying that initially students should respond orally to graphemes, lambasting the nonoral method: "The extreme type of ideational method is the so-called 'nonoral' method, where children are not required to pronounce words, but to respond directly to the content. They are shown a printed sentence such as *Skip around the room*, and the correct answer is not to say anything, but to perform the indicated act. Nothing could be less in accord with the nature of our system of writing or with the reading process such as, in the end, it must be acquired" (14). He goes on to criticize educators who teach by what he calls guesswork rather than according to such scientific principles as those upon which he has based his method.

In retrospect, Bloomfield's contribution to reading instruction added little to the phonics approach, which was already in widespread use at the time he was writing. Although he overcame some of the inconsistencies and irregularities of this approach, much undeserved criticism has been laid at his doorstep. For example, Ronald Wardhaugh writes: "Bloomfield emphasizes the relative unimportance of the content of what is read and claims that the child is faced with what is essentially a decoding task. The child already 'knows' the content, for, after all, he can speak the language" (15).

In making this statement, Wardhaugh apparently chooses to ignore Fries's explanation: "Bloomfield strove vigorously to avoid mentalistic terms (*concept*, *idea*, and so forth) in the statement of his linguistic materials and believed that 'Every scientific statement is made in physical terms.' But his efforts to achieve statements in physical rather than 'mentalistic' terms do not lead to the conclusion that he 'ignores meaning' or that 'he takes no account of meaning'" (16). Fries reproduces a portion of a letter Bloomfield sent him in 1945 in which he addresses this very point and makes himself quite clear, saying that he regards meaning an essential part of anything having to do with language.

CHARLES C. FRIES, LINGUISTICS, AND READING INSTRUCTION

A year after the publication of Bloomfield and Barnhart's *Let's Read* in 1961, Charles C. Fries, a linguist of standing comparable to Bloomfield's, completed his notable work *Linguistics and Reading*. As a descriptive, structural linguist, his basic approach was not world-shakingly different from Bloomfield's. Understanding the misinterpretations of Bloomfield's views about comprehension, Fries writes, "let us accept *comprehension of the meaning* as our chief objective and attempt to analyze the problems of the sharing of meanings through language" (17). He warns, however, that "the language is not the meaning or the message; .... A language is the *code of signals* through which various sequences of vocal sounds or speech acts get meaning" (18). He goes on to cite William S. Gray, speaking for the committee that composed the *Second Report of the National Committee on Reading*, in his statement that "reading, as here conceived, includes not only recognition, comprehension, and interpretation, but also the application of the facts apprehended in the study of personal and social problems" (19), leaving no doubt whatsoever that the reading establishment had taken its stand on the question of comprehension and implying that Fries found this stand neither distasteful nor inconsistent with his own.

Fries contends, "The process of learning to read in one's native language is *the process of transfer* from the auditory signs for language sig-

94

nals which the child has already learned, to the new visual signs for the same signals'' (20). His system of teaching was predicated on the idea of transfer and was quite behavioristic: "Learning to read . . . means developing a *considerable range of habitual responses* to a specific set of patterns of graphic shapes." He goes on to state a salient pedagogical principle: "The *teaching* of beginning reading to children of four or five must be conceived, not in terms of imparting knowledge, but in terms of opportunities for practice" (21).

Fries gives considerable attention to the sequence of the time and space dimensions involved in initial reading instruction. The time dimension is largely related to intonation (junctures) in speech, and children must be trained, through Fries's *process of transfer*, to recognize the time dimensions in the printed word. The major space dimension has to do with the fact that English is written horizontally from left to right. This is basic information that anyone who wants to read English must recognize. Also, the directional sequence has to do with the recognition of letters, all but a few of which (*H, I, O,* and *X*) must be right side up to have meaning and to be readable in any accurate way.

Fries uses only capital block letters in initial reading instruction, thereby relieving the beginning reader of the somewhat complicated problem of distinguishing letters from each other in both upper and lower case. While he contends that students must be able to distinguish individual letters in the initial stages of reading, Fries does not feel that it is entirely necessary for students to know the names of the letters; recognition is all that counts. He classifies all letters as "stroke letters" (A, E, F, H, I, K, L, M, N, T, V, W, X, Y, and Z), "circle letters" (C, G, O, Q, and S), or "stroke and circle letters" (B, D, J, P, R, and U). He teaches the most commonly used letters initially (omitting Q, Z, X, V, and J) and teaches them contrastively in relation to shape. He calls the initial reading time the "early transfer stage" and at this point introduces as little as students need in order to get along in early reading. From a group of 12 letters, Fries composes 35 words typically found in the vocabularies of five-year-olds; he limits early readings to these words and these letters. Like Bloomfield, he introduces the article *a* at this point, even though it is irregular in its pronunciation. He differs from Bloomfield in that, although *a* is the only vowel he introduces, he presents it in words that require it to be pronounced inconsistently—FAT, MAN, BAD, etc. His system emphasizes the contrastive use of minimal pairs.

Fries differentiates substantially among the terms *phonics, phonetics,* and *phonemics,* devoting Chapter 6 of *Linguistics and Reading* to this differentiation in great detail. Although one interested in this matter should turn to the actual source, it may be useful here to present Fries's succinct differentiations:

Phonics has been and continues to be a way of teaching beginning reading.

Phonetics is a set of techniques by which to identify and describe, in absolute terms, all the differences of sound features that occur in any language.

Phonemics is a set of techniques by which to identify and describe, especially in terms of distribution, the bundles of sound contrasts that constitute the structural units that mark the word patterns (22).

THE STRUCTURALISTS' CONTRIBUTIONS

From linguists like Bloomfield and Fries have come essentially more systematic ways to teach phonics. In 1968, Kenneth Goodman wrote, "What has come to represent the linguistic approach is the kind of updated phonics Bloomfield and Fries devised." Goodman identified one of the major weaknesses of the way linguists of the Bloomfield-Fries era approached the teaching of reading, but he places the blame on those in reading who asked linguists "the wrong question: How should reading be taught? They [the linguists] responded with the wrong answer though it was a linguistic one. Linguists should have been asked, 'What do you know about language that will help one understand how reading should be taught?'" (23)

The transformational-generative grammarians, led by Noam Chomsky whose *Syntactic Structures* brought about a revolution in the way many linguists view language and language learning, have spawned a new school of specialists concerned with reading instruction from a linguistic point of view. Psycholinguists Kenneth Goodman and Yetta Goodman have offered valuable insights to teachers who need to understand how language operates and how reading instruction is related to the psychological processes involved in language learning. The pioneering work the Goodmans have undertaken in miscue analysis has broad implications for every reading teacher at every level of education and is the subject of the next chapter.

Chapter 9
LEARNING FROM MISREADINGS: A LOOK AT MISCUE ANALYSIS (1)

In 1969, Ronald Wardhaugh wrote: "There is something very important missing from the work that has been done so far in applying linguistic knowledge acquired over the past decade. The kind of linguistics which is partially introduced into some versions of the linguistic method is Bloomfieldian linguistics; however, beginning with the publication of Chomsky's *Syntactic Structures* (2) in 1957, linguistics has undergone a revolution." Wardhaugh continues, "It would not be fair to say that Bloomfieldian linguistics is dead or even moribund; but, to use the current idiom, it is not where the action is" (3).

Wardhaugh goes on to applaud the new linguists, the transformational-generative grammarians, because of their interest in making "a distinction between the skills and competency a person must have to behave linguistically and his actual observed linguistic behavior" (4). Wardhaugh then speculates on some of the ways in which the transformational-generative grammarians might shed light on the teaching of reading and suggests, quite prophetically as it turns out, "Even mistakes should be thought of as applications of wrong rules, as evidence of faulty processing, rather than as instances of random behavior" (5). Wardhaugh cannot be credited, because of this statement, with fathering the miscue analysis movement, inasmuch as Kenneth Goodman and Yetta Goodman were already beginning their investigations in this area and were applying some of the fruits of the transformational-generative grammarians to their research. Kenneth Goodman had also already published *The Psycholinguistic Nature of the Reading Process* (6), and Wardhaugh was certainly familiar with this important book.

In the three decades since the publication of *Syntactic Structures*, Chomsky's impact has been felt in many areas of learning and investigation. His exploration into the question of how all the syntactic structures of any language are generated from basic kernel sentences has focused attention on the underlying psychology of syntactic generation and has inaugurated the intensive study of psycholinguistics.

As psycholinguists have turned their attention to areas of human communication previously unexplored from a psycholinguistic standpoint, they have developed a new and broader understanding of language skills. Many of the emerging researchers in this area have come to realize that the acquisition of language skills, notably of reading and writing, follows psycholinguistic patterns that fit into generalizable categories. Subsequent research has provided many challenging insights into the patterns of language learning; however, some of the most important research has, because of its specialized nature and difficulty of interpretation and understanding, failed to reach classroom teachers who could profit significantly from many of its findings.

MISCUE ANALYSIS DEFINED

Kenneth Goodman coined the term *miscue analysis* as an outgrowth of his investigation into the sorts of errors students make in oral reading and what these errors reveal about the reading characteristics of the people who make them. A miscue, as Goodman uses the term, is merely an error or inaccuracy in either oral or silent reading. Goodman elects to use the term *miscue* because "miscues are not simply errors, but the results of the reading process having miscarried in some minor or major ways." Goodman continues, "The phenomena to be dealt with will be called miscues, rather than errors, in order to avoid the negative connotation of errors (all miscues are not bad) and to avoid the implication that good reading does not include miscues" (7).

Teachers can learn a great deal from the miscues their students make in oral reading. Although they can assess miscues only in oral reading, these miscues can certainly suggest the types of problems their students are having in silent reading as well. It is important that teachers heed Goodman's admonition "that only in rare special circumstances is oral reading free of miscues and that silent reading is never miscue-free" (8). More importantly, the teachers must hearken to Goodman's research-based caveat that "it appears likely that a reader who requires perfection in his reading will be a rather inefficient reader" (9). The faster most people read, the more miscues they make.

PROCESSING GRAPHO-PHONIC, SYNTACTIC, AND SEMANTIC INFORMATION

According to Goodman, when readers react to graphic displays (writing) on a page, they must process three types of information: graphophonic, syntactic, and semantic. Sometimes they must process all three types of information simultaneously, sometimes not. They process syntactic information as syntactic structures such as phrases, clauses, etc. For example, a reader who reads "nip" for "pin" or, more commonly in oral reading and speaking, the metathesized "irrevelancy" for "irrelevancy" is processing grapho-phonic and, possibly, semantic information, whereas the reader who renders "They have done a good day's work" as "They had did a good day's work" is processing syntactic information and probably is miscuing because of dialect interference.

Students who are reading silently are decoding (translating) graphic markings on a page into meaningful units. Probably the most efficient readers—that is, those in the top 1 or 2 percent nationally in reading ability and reading efficiency—are engaged largely in a decoding process. Yet even these readers, in their silent reading, engage in some subvocalization. Any vocalization, whether reading aloud or subvocalizing in silent reading, involves a more complicated process than mere decoding; it requires decoding of the graphic representation and then encoding of the sound for which the graphic representation stands. This process slows readers down, although in some cases it may not work much to the detriment of their efficiency. Readers who encounter new words (*miniseries*, *subarea*, *kinesics*) or complicated words (*Zoroastrianism*, *shenanigan*, *neuropsychiatric*) for the first time usually have to vocalize them in order to be able to deal with them. If they are not dealing with them within a context, then their reading efficiency (comprehension) is reduced.

On the other hand, some readers need to vocalize every word in silent reading, and in so doing, some of them slow their reading pace to the point that they cannot derive the meaning from a paragraph or, perhaps, even from a sentence or a phrase. It is important for the teacher of reading to recognize the kinds of processes that are going on in reading and, having identified them, to know how to use them diagnostically to determine what is most likely to help individual students.

TWO BASIC CATEGORIES OF MISCUING

Although Goodman has identified 28 different categories of miscues (10), let us consider at this point two major areas in which miscues are detected and consider further how teachers can use the information that these miscues provide to determine the type and gravity of the reading problems students have.

Frank Smith (11) (as well as Goodman (12), Carolyn L. Burke and Goodman (13), and Rose-Marie Weber (14)) notes that proficient beginning readers make as many miscues as beginning readers who are not proficient, but that their miscues are of a different nature from those made by their less proficient classmates. He reports: "The errors of less proficient readers typically reflect a good deal of the graphic information in the written text (for example, 'saw' for 'was,' 'butter' for 'batter') but they make little sense in the context of the passage as a whole. More accomplished readers sometimes make errors that may appear quite gross visually—omitting, substituting, or rearranging entire sequences of words—but that nonetheless retain the underlying meaning of the passage they are reading. They do not stop to sound out or even identify individual words" (15).

Obviously, the student who reads, "She went to a moving in wont" for "She went to a movie in town" and goes right on reading has a much greater and more disabling reading problem than does the student who reads, "There is some*one* in the house" for "There is some*body* in the house," or "They live happily in the forest" for "They live in the forest happily." The latter reader is also distinguishable from the former because he or she, in making a miscue like "She crust the day she was born," will go back and reread, "She curst the day she was born," realizing that the first rendering of the sentence does not make sense.

In determining the extent and type of students' reading problems, teachers must pay careful attention to what happens when students are reading orally. They must also bear in mind Goodman's comment that readers who demand perfection of themselves are likely to be inefficient readers.

READING AS INFORMATION PROCESSING

In one of his early articles, Goodman writes, "A proficient reader is one so efficient in sampling and predicting that he uses the least (not the most) available information necessary" (16). In other words, really proficient readers can comprehend accurately what they are reading without laboring over it. The eye feeds the graphic representation to the mind which instantly, and in many cases nonverbally, processes it. The flow to the mind is constant and rapid; the units communicated are relatively large units: "secondary school," or even "scdryschol" rather than "secon-da-ry sc-ho-ol" or "s-e-c-o-n-d-a-r-y s-c-h-o-o-l." Proficient readers are probably engaging the right hemisphere of the brain as well as the left in the reading process, allowing the gestalt of words and phrases to aid in their processing for greater efficiency and accuracy.

Goodman calls reading "a psycholinguistic process, in which meaning is decoded from a linguistic medium of communication" (17). This linguistic medium of communication is presumably graphic representation or writing unless one wishes to go so far as to say that deriving meaning from a painting, let us say, is a form of reading. Goodman's definition would be quite commonplace—in essence, "Reading is decoding writing"—were it not for the inclusion of the words "psycholinguistic process." These words move the definition into new territory, which is very much concerned with the question of how the mind works on language and with the converse question of how language works on the mind. It is this qualification that makes Goodman's definition unique and that should lead teachers to a greater awareness of the learning problems some of their students have. The student who is able to see in the mind's eye "secondary school" or "secondaryschool" can process that piece of information 15 times faster than the student who sees "s-e-c-o-n-d-a-r-y s-c-h-o-o-l." And, perhaps more importantly, the former student has the mental concept of "secondary school" in mind when he or she pushes on to the next word or phrase. The latter student moves on to the next word or phrase in the same laborious way that he or she attacked "s-e-c-o-n-d-a-r-y s-c-h-o-o-l" and cannot derive meaning from the material being read. Such a student is, for all practical purposes, a nonreader.

Teachers beyond the primary grades who encounter such students are faced with enormous problems, some of them stemming from early training that stressed a narrow phonics emphasis over the reading of whole words. For some students, the early damage may be all but irreversible. For others, new approaches to reading—and these new approaches must involve a great deal of eye training—may yield results. A first step would be to surround such students with large signs, clearly printed, identifying objects around the classroom—desk, door, chair, window, clock, etc.—and to engage them in games involving words. For example, on large cards, clearly printed commands such as "Look Left" or "Stand Up" or "Touch Your Nose" might be written. The teacher flashes a card. The first student to obey the command gets to flash the next card. Such activities will encourage some students to see and process larger entities than they have been able to process previously. If students cannot handle commands, the teacher can try writing just one word on each card and begin by saying, "Touch whatever part of you is written on the card"; then she or he would flash *ear*, *nose*, *chin*, *eye*, and *toe*, and graduate to *wrist*, *ankle*, *finger*, *stomach*, and other more difficult words. The teacher might start another exercise by saying, "Point to whatever is written on the card," and continue with words such as *door*, *wall*, *floor*, *boy*, and *desk*, and then proceed to more difficult words like *light*, *ceiling*, *eraser*, *cupboards*, and *chalkboard*.

Teachers must remember that post-primary school students who have severe reading deficits are ashamed of those deficits. Their shame may manifest itself in various ways—apathy, defensiveness, or lack of cooperation. Characteristically such students have learned not to take risks in the school setting because in the past their taking risks has resulted in penalties. If anything is to succeed in helping them to cope with and overcome their problems, it must be presented to them in contexts that are neither threatening nor judgmental. In the excitement of a game, students lose their self-consciousness and perform more effectively than they would in a more typical classroom setting.

READING MISCUES AND DIALECTS

Teachers working with students brought up in environments where dialects that vary significantly from so-called Standard English predominate must have some understanding of their students' dialects if they are to judge whether students are actually miscuing in oral reading or whether they are merely making substitutions from their own dialects. In most rural areas of Piedmont, North Carolina, for example, a student who reads, "Maybe I can go if the rain stops" as "I might can go if the rain stops" is translating the more standard expression into the dialect of the region. W. Nelson Francis has noted that students whose dialects differ greatly from that in the works they are trying to read (usually something close to Network Standard English) may have trouble learning to read (18). However, the child whose teacher knows some of the dialects of the community will stand a better chance of learning to read than the child whose teacher is ignorant of these dialects (19).

Kenneth R. Johnson has made useful generalizations about sounds that Black children use in certain words, particularly those words ending in /th/ such as *birth*, which in Black dialect is *birf*. He has also noted other consistent patterns that teachers of reading should recognize (20). Johnson reminds the reader that "Black English is *not* 'sloppy' English spoken by children with 'lazy lips and lazy tongues'; it is a structured, functional variety of English, and it should not be stigmatized" (21). What Johnson says about Black dialect may be said with equal validity about other dialects of English.

Teachers need to recognize that students may make substitutions into their own dialects. William Labov notes, "If a student reads *He always looked for trouble when he read the news* as *He a'way look' fo' trouble when he read* (rhyming with *bed*) *de news*, the teacher should be able to judge that he is reading correctly " (22). Such a rendering is reading correctly *within the confines and pronunciation system of a student's own dialect*. Teachers also need to remember that if the task at hand is to teach reading to students who are having difficulty mastering this skill, *the focus should be on reading*. If the student reads "have did" for "have done," this is not the time for a grammar lesson which would only divert student attention from the task at hand. In trying to teach several things at once, teachers reduce the efficiency with which slower students learn.

One might bear in mind a sequence in Dorothy Heathcote's film *Three Looms Waiting* (23), in which she is helping students to enact a prisoner-of-war scene. She tells the students that as prisoners-of-war, they will be grilled by their captors. Then she begins grilling a boy: "What work did you do before the war?" "I was a lorry driver." "Is your father alive?" "No, Ma'am." "How did he die?" "He was killed in the war, ma'am." "Where did he live?" "In London." "Where in London?" "Coventry, ma'am." "And is your mother alive?"

In the critique that followed this session, Heathcote was asked, "Why did you not tell the boy that Coventry is not a part of London?" She replied, "Because I don't give a damn where Coventry is. I was not giving a geography lesson. I was trying to help a young boy to know what it feels like to be a prisoner, an alien in a foreign land, and at that moment he was beginning to know what it felt like. I could not interrupt the development of this feeling to tell him where Coventry is." Too many teachers forget that focus can be destroyed if the lesson deviates from its intended objective(s) in order to provide information that the student does not need at that particular moment.

Teachers of reading need to remember Goodman's words: "(1) phonemes do not really exist outside of the full system of restraints in which they are found [and] (2) oral language is no less a code than written language" (24). Indeed, when oral response is produced from graphic representation (reading from printed material), the reader is involved in a psychologically complex process and is called upon to juggle two or more coding challenges simultaneously. Although the process is an easy and natural one for proficient readers (which most teachers are and have been since their earliest recollections), reading can be an incredibly difficult, intimidating, and discouraging process for the deficient reader. If teachers do not understand this fully (and it is difficult to understand why others have trouble doing the things that one does easily and well), they are not in a position to teach reading to people with reading handicaps.

TEACHER FEEDBACK AND MISCUES

Since 1975, considerable attention has been paid to analyzing the kinds of feedback that teachers give students who make miscues when they read aloud. R. L. Allington finds that teachers interrupt poor readers at the point of a miscue more frequently than they interrupt good readers and that the most frequent interruption occurs when the teacher corrects the miscue by supplying the needed word. Teachers also cue poor readers to graphemic clues slightly more often than they do good readers. He concludes that the differential (and sometimes deferential) treatment accorded poor readers may contribute to their problems in reading rather than helping them (25).

Working from the Allington study, a group of researchers at the University of Texas at Austin conclude from their extended observations of 22 second grade teachers that "in guided oral reading, the teacher does little to encourage the poor reader to begin to look like the good" (26). They recommend that poor readers be given materials in which their error rates will be low so that they will begin to gain a better image of themselves as readers. They advocate not doing round-robin reading in class, but replacing this activity with the soft reading of stories so that teachers can offer them feedback privately rather than in front of the whole class. They also urge teachers to wait until the end of the sentence—or better until the end of the paragraph—before they interrupt students.

The University of Texas researchers place emphasis on reading for meaning. They suggest that teachers be tolerant of miscues that do not affect meaning and that their initial response to miscues be "on the meaning level, asking the student to reread the sentence with the miscue and/or asking if what the student has said makes sense" (27). Certainly at the early level of reading instruction that concerns these researchers, a major consideration should be with finding ways to help students succeed. If they do not have a sense of success in reading at this level, they may be deficient readers throughout their lifetimes.

USING JUDGMENT IN DEALING WITH MISCUES

Miscues are a natural part of all reading, oral and silent. If the aim in oral reading is perfection, then every miscue or error must be corrected. However, to do this will discourage students and will do little to help them become better readers. Rather, it will destroy in them any desire to read. Teachers need to be quick to recognize the types of miscues students make and to know that some require attention while others do not. James Peter Tortelli writes, "Since most readers are speakers of the language they read, they bring to the process of reading an intuitive knowledge of oral language that facilitates their getting meaning from written language" (28).

Probably the best criterion teachers can apply in reaching decisions about whether to correct students' miscues is that of meaning: Does the reader understand what he/she is reading? The oral language that students are accustomed to hearing may differ quite substantially from the written language to which they are exposed in reading. Many students, while they are decoding from the printed page, are simultaneously encoding into their own dialects, making the Standard English on the page conform systematically to the conventions of those dialects. On a rather simple level, *ten* may come out *tin*, not because the reader cannot differentiate between the two words of this minimal pair but because he or she does not make an audible distinction in his or her normal pronunciation of the two words. In such situations, even though both words may be pronounced identically, context will reveal which is intended. On a more sophisticated level, Standard English "it does" or "she doesn't" may come out "it do" or "she don't" (or even "she don'") because the reader will translate the standard expression into the corresponding locution in dialect. Such a deviation from the printed text is not an error to be corrected *if the purpose of oral reading is to determine whether the reader is able to read a text with meaning*. Teaching the differences that exist among dialects may be appropriate ultimately in a student's linguistic development, but teachers need to learn not to confuse students by drifting spontaneously into teaching a second major lesson because something being done in the primary major lesson suggests doing so.

Laray Brown writes of a Black child who made no differentiation between *him* and *hem* in oral reading, pronouncing both words /him/. Brown asks, "Did he mispronounce all words with these two vowels in similar environments—for example, *pin* and *pen*?" Brown continues: "The answer was yes. Consequently, I said that I would not have corrected the Black child and that I would have corrected the White child [making the same miscue]. I feel that one must consider with which language system one is working, the Black English (BE) or the Standard English (SE) system" (29). While many traditionalists rebel against this point of view, it is linguistically and pedagogically sound. The question is not whether so-called standard usage (Network Standard) *should* be taught; eventually students obviously will profit from being introduced to it. However, in the initial stages of reading instruction, the focus should be on decoding and comprehending, not on the subtleties of dialect differences.

Brown contends that speakers of dialects such as Black English have a passive knowledge and understanding of Standard English sufficient for them to be able to comprehend it. He cites tests "where children were asked to repeat sentences that they were given orally [in which] Black children 'digested' the given SE forms and rendered translations in BE with the same meaning." Therefore, Brown contends that "failure of some Black children to learn to read is not due primarily to dialectal differences. I see no reason that a child needs to have more than a passive knowledge of SE to learn to read" (30).

Emotions concerning this issue have run so high that the results of reliable and meticulous linguistic studies have been obscured by the emotional involvement of teachers and parents who feel that every language problem must be worked on simultaneously, despite the existence of convincing research evidence that learning will be diminished when this is done.

Aaron Lipton substantiates the fact that "as children call out substituted words, they *may* actually *see* and *know* the words as they are written, but find it more linguistically comfortable to say the words as they do." Lipton warns: "In many instances in forcing a child to call words accurately by continual reference to his errors and correction of them, we deny him the opportunity to read within the framework of his own language development. This condition has caused many children to avoid reading and to become failures with the reading process" (31).

Neither Brown nor Lipton nor this writer believes that any child should be locked into one dialect for the whole of his or her educational experience. The plea is that children be allowed the right to their own language while they are trying to master the elementary forms of some of the basic skills of that language. When children can function unself-consciously in the areas of speaking, reading, and writing, teachers can profitably turn their attention to questions of the different usages and conventions that exist within the broad range of English language dialects.

GAINING INFORMATION THROUGH MISCUES

Perceptive teachers will learn a great deal about their students' ability to cope with language if they know how to interpret the miscues their students make in oral reading. It takes linguistic sophistication to read and simultaneously translate into another dialect, and many primary school students are easily able to do this. Such linguistic flexibility should be valued rather than condemned.

Tortelli recommends that primary teachers make individual diagnoses of their students by having each student read aloud to them an unfamiliar story of which the teacher has a copy. The teacher is to write on his other copy every word the student utters that is not in the original text or that differs from the original. Omissions of words are also to be noted.

First, the teacher places horizontally on a sheet of paper four column headings: "Unexpected Readings" (substitution of words or any other deviatons from the text), "Intended Readings," "Language," and "Meaning." He or she then numbers the paper vertically from 1 to 10, and the first 10 unexpected calls are recorded. If the student reads "hurt" for "hit" as the verb in the first sentence, "A big boy hit Nan," then "hurt" is recorded in column 1, "Unexpected Readings." The word "hit" is recorded in column 2, "Intended Readings." In column 3 a "yes" is recorded because the substitution has resulted in a grammatically acceptable sentence. In most cases "A big boy hit Nan" could be rendered "A big boy hurt Nan" with little grammatical problem; however, "Them big boy hit/hurt Nan" might indicate a grammatical inconsistency (depending on the reader's dialect), indicating that the reader has made a miscue that is not meaningful in terms of the sense of the sentence. In column 4, "Meaning," a "no" is recorded if either the word "Them" or the word "hurt" has been the substitution because the original meaning would not be conveyed in either case (32).

In order to obtain the most valid information from students who read to teachers individually, Goodman recommends that the reading should be somewhat difficult for the student, a bit above his or her level, and that it should be long enough to generate 25 or more miscues. Goodman would have the reading recorded for later replay; he would also have the student retell the story immediately after having read it to check for comprehension. The miscues would be coded with the use of *Taxonomy*, *Reading Miscue Inventory*, or other such means so that they might be viewed analytically and diagnosed according to the student's geographical origins or ethnic background (33).

107

Goodman's suggestion should be followed with caution, however, as the more recent findings of the University of Texas researchers indicate. Perhaps after children are somewhat secure in their reading, Goodman's plan can be used for diagnostic purposes; it should, however, be used sparingly and only after students have developed the sort of self-image that such diagnostic work will not erode.

LEVELS OF MISCUING

Teachers should always pay close attention to the levels of miscuing. Calling "don't" for "do not" is not a serious miscue. It will not distort meaning even though it may alter in some minute way the style of what the student is reading. If a beginning reader pronounces a word in dialect (*idear* for *idea*), the miscue is hardly worth considering. An inability to distinguish consistently between *them* and *they* or between *him* and *his* is a problem of greater magnitude because it usually will alter meaning. Omitting words, particularly descriptive words such as reading "A boy hit the girl" rather than "A big boy hit the girl," may, if not checked, cause future problems in comprehension. Misreading "was" as "saw" may, if done consistently, indicate problems connected with mixed dominance, a common cause of serious reading handicaps. Difficulty in distinguishing between "m" and "w" may suggest a similar problem. Reading "brain" for "train" is more serious than reading "goin'" for "going," "gonna" for "going to," or "wanna" for "want to."

Teachers in time come to know their students well enough to be able to judge their reading performances in the broad contexts of their lives and environments. No single set of criteria will work for all children, obviously. It is the teacher's job—and a great challenge it is—to be able to assess the individual situations of all the students in the classroom and to work with all these students to help them overcome the specific stumbling blocks that stand between them and the highest level of achievement of which each is capable.

HOW TO USE INFORMATION GAINED
FROM ANALYSIS OF MISCUES

Armed with an understanding of how to categorize miscues in oral reading, teachers can begin to classify the types of reading problems that many of their students have. They can also make certain broad decisions about which students have reading problems that may legitimately handicap them and which students, even though they make miscues, derive the basic meaning from most of what they read and read it with sufficient speed and efficiency that they can be considered adequate readers.

Gerard M. Ryan classifies miscues as *quantitative* or *qualitative*. He considers quantitative miscues to include "five major response categories, viz., substitutions, omissions, insertions, reversals and repetitions of an item or a group of items." His qualitative miscues are based upon graphic similarities, grammatical function, correction, syntactic acceptability, semantic acceptability, and change in meaning (34). This classification, or one that individual teachers devise for their own situations, can be extremely useful in helping teachers to make an accurate assessment of what specific kinds of miscues their students are making.

Yetta Goodman writes: "There is no question that certain types of miscues are of higher order than others; miscues of low order give way to miscues of higher order as children become more proficient readers. Miscues must not be looked upon as mistakes that are bad and should be eradicated but as overt behaviors which may unlock aspects of intellectual processing. . . . Miscues in reading give insight into the reading process" (35). But if miscues are to provide teachers with insights into the reading process, then teachers must have a sophisticated knowledge of how and why the student is miscuing. They must know when correction is appropriate and when it is not.

Teachers must also seek to provide their students with ideas and concepts at their maturity level as the process of teaching reading advances. Because they are not dependent on reading skills, frequent discussion activities allow students with reading deficits to function in situations in which they can experience a feeling of success and accomplishment. This sense of accomplishment may encourage them to put forth the extra effort necessary to become efficient readers.

Chapter 10
DIALECTS AND EARLY
READING INSTRUCTION

We learned in the preceding chapter on miscue analysis that probably no efficient sustained reading, oral or silent, is wholly free from miscues. Using the least rather than the most information available to differentiate one word from another leads to efficient reading habits; it also makes miscues inevitable. Written English is, in itself, a unique dialect, quite different in many particulars from any form of spoken English. English written in the so-called Standard Dialect, however, bears closer resemblances to spoken language of the same dialect than it does to, let us say, southern dialect, New England dialect, or any other dialect of English. These resemblances are true at both the letter-sound (graphemic-phonemic) and syntactic levels.

DIALECTS AND STATUS

Linguists have amply demonstrated that all the established dialects they have studied follow consistent patterns, no matter how much at variance such patterns might be with those found in the version of the mother language spoken by those who control society (1). They contend that every language, as well as every dialect of language, meets the communication needs of the group using it. Whatever the controlling class speaks comes to be viewed as standard. As power shifts, fashions change. For example, French was the polite language in England from the time of the Norman conquest until some two or three centuries later; English was held in low regard, as were those who spoke it.

The election of John Kennedy to the presidency added status to a New England dialect, which was already well accepted because that region of the country has provided many of our nation's leaders. The aura surrounding the New England dialect is an aura of power.

Jimmy Carter's rise to the presidency caused many people to have a more tolerant attitude than was common a quarter of a century ago toward the southern dialect commonly used in rural Georgia. British English, which is as deviant from the Network Standard Dialect of the United States as Black English is, is favorably received by most Americans for so complex a variety of psychological and social reasons that to chart them in any exhaustive way would be difficult.

It is interesting to note that in London or Leeds or Liverpool, the Scottish dialect stigmatizes its users just as Black dialect can stigmatize its users in some white middle-class environments in the United States. The same Americans who show a negative emotional reaction to Black dialect might be charmed by the very Scottish dialect that makes a proper Londoner cringe. Such reactions are not usually logical, although some history usually exists to account for them, and this history often reaches far back into ill-remembered time. We all carry with us language prejudices, both pro and con, that we cannot begin to understand—or even, in some cases, to recognize.

THE KING CASE

The case of *Martin Luther King Junior Elementary School Children et al.* v. *Ann Arbor School District Board* has considerable relevance for all speakers of major dialects in the United States. This action was brought against the Ann Arbor School Board by 11 Black elementary school children who contended that they were not being provided equal opportunity to learn because the people teaching them did not know enough about their dialect, Black English, to provide them with the means of learning Standard English and the basic communication skills society demands. The complaint read in part: "This case is not an effort on the part of the plaintiffs to require that they be taught 'black English' or that their instruction throughout their schooling be in 'black English,' or that a dual language program be provided. . . . It is a straightforward effort to require the court to intervene on the children's behalf to require the defendant School District Board to take the appropriate action to teach them to read in the standard English of the school, the commercial world, the arts, science, and professions" (2).

The plaintiffs' case was supported by an impressive array of expert witnesses that included Daniel Fader, Geneva Smitherman, William Labov, J. L. Dillard, Ronald Edmonds, Richard Bailey, and numerous other linguists and educators, all of whom substantiated the validity of viewing Black English as a systematic dialect about which specific linguistic generalizations can be made. A summary of these generalizations is published in the decision (3).

The court ultimately found that the defendant school district had a responsibility to provide its teachers with training in Black English so that they might better understand the language backgrounds of the plaintiffs, thereby enabling them to teach these children basic communication skills—reading, in particular—more effectively. The district was ordered to make provision for in-service training of its teachers in the dialect of the plaintiffs.

The King case is important because it establishes legally the fact that Black English is a systematic language system and that students who are taught by teachers ignorant of this system are denied the equal treatment that the Constitution guarantees them. The case, of course, has broad implications for speakers of all dialects, not just of Black English.

BLACK DIALECT

Linguists have long realized that Black English is a legitimate and systematic form of the English language, and the King case certainly demonstrates the validity of this judgment in no uncertain terms. The valid grammatical generalizations that were made in the court decision about its structure, conventions, and use echoed much that linguists like Labov, Smitherman, and Dillard had been writing for years (4). Among these generalizations are the following:

1. Omission of *-s* in possessives: *That is my sister book. Where Mary car at?*

2. Regularization of third person singular: *That dude run real fast. Do he have my check?*

3. Regularization of strong verbs: *throwed* for *threw*, *have did* for *have done*.

4. Dropping of *-s* after a plural marker: *Hey, Ollie, can I have ten cent? Those (Dose) three dude be crazy.* In the second example, notice the double plural markers, *Those* and *three*. Also note that Standard Dialect omits the plural *-s* in some situations: *I want a ten cent candy bar. Do you have a fifty cent piece?* but not in others: *Give me fifty cents.*

5. Omission of terminal *-ed* in the past tense: *Lawdy, I cook all day last Sunday. I fix that screen door yesterday.* Again, note the avoidance of redundancy.

6. Rendering of the conditional indirect question: *Alice ask can she come to the party*, not *Alice asked if she could come to the party.*

7. Use of the *be* copula rather than *is*: *I be here every day till closing time.* The copula may also be omitted (deleted zero form), but this is done only where Standard English would use a contraction. Black English may use the contraction, but it more often omits the copula: *He's going home* may be rendered as it stands, but more usually in Black English it will be rendered *He goin' home* or *He be goin' home.* The deletion never occurs in instances where Standard English cannot accommodate a contraction: *I don't know where he is* cannot, in Standard English, be *I don't know where he's*; hence, in Black English it would consistently be rendered *I don't know where he at* or *I don't know where he be* (5).

8. Omission of the copula: *Where John brother at? There (Dere) my house. Man, you in my seat.*

9. Dropping of prefixes: *'til* for *until*; *'zausted* for *exhausted*; *'spired* for *inspired*.

10. Omission of final consonants *k*, *p*, and *t* preceded by *s*: *desk, pest,* and *lisp* become *des', pes',* and *lis'*.

11. Substitution of /f/ for /th/ in words like *with* (*wif*) and *teeth* (*teef*).

12. Substitution of /d/ or /t/ for initial /th/: *dere* for *there*; *does* for *those*; *trew* for *through* or *threw* (6).

13. Subject reiteration: *Jessie, she come to see me. My mama, she a big lady. Mary car, it won' go.*

The foregoing usages are standard within the dialect context in which they occur. This does not make them acceptable in or appropriate to all situations; however, linguistically speaking, they are neither correct nor incorrect. They fulfill the criterion of intelligibility to other speakers of the same dialect. They permit communication. Any judgments about their correctness would necessarily be social rather than linguistic. While social judgments cannot be ignored, neither can they be permitted to cloud the situation in planning early language learning experiences such as initial reading instruction.

COMMON SENSE WOULD TELL YOU

Common sense suggests that in the early stages of reading instruction, children whose dialects are dramatically different from the Standard English used in the materials they are expected to read might learn much more effectively from early reading materials in their own dialects. Written English is, after all, a dialectal variant of spoken English. It seems reasonable to assume that children who have to deal with the inherent dialectal variations between Standard English and both the English they are most used to hearing at home and the English they themselves speak embark upon their initial reading experiences with a double disadvantage.

Linguists Joan Baratz, Roger W. Shuy, and William A. Stewart reflected on this problem, as did many of their colleagues, and made a persuasive case for the use of dialect readers for Black students in the primary grades; that is, they wanted to make available beginning textbooks in reading that present the same story in both the Black dialect and Standard English. Judy Schwartz reports, "The first practical application of this approach occurred earlier, in 1968, when the Board of Education of the City of Chicago published a series of experimental readers in which half of the content was written in Black dialect" (7). A year later, J. Steptoe published *Stevie* (8), the basic text of which is in Standard English but the dialogue of which is all in Black dialect. By the next year, the Education Study Center had published three dialect readers (9) in which stories were presented in Black dialect and Standard English. The stories were identical in every particular except the text. *Ollie* reads: "Here go Ollie./Ollie have a big family./He have three sisters./A sister name Brenda." The control volume reads: "This is Ollie./Ollie has a big family./He has three sisters./A sister named Brenda, ..."

Common sense once had people convinced that the earth was flat, that the universe was geocentric, and that people could never leave the environment of their own planet. We have lived to see all these common-sense hypotheses disproved. It is now clear that the common-sense idea of using Black dialect readers to teach reading to students who speak Black dialect has been abandoned, even though the linguistic hypotheses on which the theory rested were appealing and, to many educators, acceptable.

But before we discuss the research that has tested this hypothesis, let us consider public reaction to the introduction of dialect readers.

THE PUBLIC OUTCRY AGAINST DIALECT READERS

Emotions ran high in areas where Black dialect readers were used for initial reading instruction. Most negative reactions to dialect readers came from people who had little or no formal exposure to linguistic theory so their objections were based upon something other than linguistic considerations. Schwartz conducted a revealing attitudinal survey that focused on the reception of Black dialect materials by a sampling of 69 people categorized by occupation, race, and socioeconomic status (SES). She hypothesized that (1) those expressing favorable attitudes would be teachers and other education-related professionals, as well as white respondents of average socioeconomic status; and (2) those expressing unfavorable opinions would be nonprofessionals, Blacks, and those of low socioeconomic status (10).

Although the Schwartz study found that "the use of Black dialect materials for beginning reading instruction, especially as a transitional medium and when used in conjunction with standard dialect materials, is perceived positively by both Black and white people" (11), the researchers elicited some distinctly negative responses from the respondents: "Good English is good English, and bad English is bad English, no matter who is speaking it. There is no such thing as Black language." Schwartz writes: "Most respondents, regardless of category of occupation, race, and SES, demonstrated an incomplete or inaccurate understanding of Black dialect. Among the terms used to describe it were: broken English, the wrong way, incorrect, not proper, slang, bad English, play talk. One Black paraprofessional characterized Black English as '. . . a short easy way out'" (12). Certainly the responses suggest that people have little knowledge of the linguistic status of Black English— and probably of most other dialects of English. They are judgmental in ways that linguists are not.

Perhaps those most troubled by Black dialect materials were Black parents, many of whom felt that the future hope for their children depended on their being educated in the same way as members of mainstream American society so that they would ultimately have upward social mobility within the context of mainstream America. Reading the King case makes one aware that the plaintiffs' parents shared the views of many Black parents who spoke against the use of dialect readers in schools.

Speaking of dialect materials, Schwartz reports: "Almost as quickly as they appeared . . . they vanished from the scene usually in the midst of a heated debate in which the move to use such readers was characterized as an attempt at racial stereotyping. Typically, the strongest opponents were middle-class Blacks" (13).

Dorothy S. Strickland voiced strenuous objections to the use of dialect materials for a number of reasons, one of which was that "Most Black parents object to the use of such books as initial instructional materials for reading." She worried that the continued use of such materials threatened "the potential erosion of school/community relations and the resultant disruption in the learning process which would follow" (14). William A. Stewart answers this objection by saying, "It is difficult for me to see . . . especially given the attitudinal and cultural autonomy of lower-class Black children vis-a-vis their parents, how parental hostility to any particular teaching strategy could offset whatever in-school pedagogical advantages the teaching strategy might have" (15). This statement apparently overlooks the structure of the Black family. It suggests to this writer that Stewart would give the schools totalitarian powers to teach students as and what they like if, in the school's eyes, learning would proceed from doing so. The voices of parents, it seems he is suggesting, should not be heeded.

Strickland also expresses an understandable concern about Black dialect readers because there is not a single Black dialect "which all Black disadvantaged children speak" (16). She is not opposed to using dialect materials in classrooms, but she suggests that initial reading materials be "based on the individual child's own language. . . . Personal experience stories using the child's dictation as the content and the teacher as scribe can serve as an important tool for introducing reading" (17).

Such an exercise might be taken one step further. Teachers or other students might translate such stories "the way Johnny or Mary or Sandra or Mark would tell them." In classes that are racially and culturally diverse, this sort of exercise is enormously valuable because it involves students in working with point of view, with language and syntactic variety, and with authentic revising, one of the most sophisticated and productive forms of which is that of preparing a story for a different audience than that for which it was originally written.

DO DIALECT READERS HELP STUDENTS?

Research on the effectiveness of dialect readers is still insufficient to support any sweeping generalizations about their overall usefulness to dialect speakers who are learning to read. As was noted in the preceding chapter, a passive understanding of Standard English appears to be all that dialect speakers need in order to learn how to read. While acknowledging the difference between Standard English and Black English, Jane Torrey concludes: "The difference in phonology between Standard English and Black English is not directly relevant to reading. *All* children who learn to read English have to break a fairly complex code of sound-spelling relationships. The fact that the correspondences are different for speakers of Afro-American does not in itself prove that they are more difficult than for standard speakers" (18). Torrey's thesis is "that the functional aspects of language have more serious implications for illiteracy than the structural ones." She goes on, "A passive understanding of standard dialect should suffice for purposes of learning to read, *even if a given child never learns to use the standard forms of speech*" (19).

It should be remembered, for example, that most southern students entering school are exposed to reading materials in a dialect other than their natural one, yet their passive understanding of the version of English found in their initial reading materials is sufficient to enable them to read the materials at hand. This writer is aware of no serious suggestions that initial reading materials be prepared in southern, midwestern, or New England dialect, and the absence of such suggestions stems from the fact that it has long been recognized that students speaking such dialects can make the transfer to the language of their initial readers because their passive understanding of Standard English is sufficient to permit this transfer (20).

Herbert D. Simons and Kenneth R. Johnson (the latter a native speaker of Black English) report on a research study of 67 second and third grade Black children in Oakland, California, all of whom were users of some form of the Black English dialect. The study considers many aspects of dialect interference in early reading experiences. Although this study deals with too small a sample to be viewed as conclusive, it "provides no evidence that second and third grade dialect-speaking Black children read dialect texts any better than they read standard texts" (21). This single conclusion, the most important one the researchers reach in the study, flies in the face of what many prominent linguists have believed and runs quite contrary to what this writer would have expected such research to reveal. It is clear that the need exists for more research of this kind and that it should involve a larger and more diverse sampling. Simons and Johnson's materials provide a significant initial step, and their findings are important.

RECOGNIZING THE LANGUAGE ABILITIES OF DIALECT SPEAKERS

Researchers have asked whether disadvantaged dialect speakers begin school with sufficient command of oral language to make initial reading instruction feasible for them. Martin Deutsch contended in 1963 that failure in reading among disadvantaged children is attributable to their having had insufficient experiences with vocabulary and syntax (22). Some years later, S. Engelmann contended that the average child from a low socioeconomic background has no linguistic concepts and cannot understand the meaning of common words (23). More recently, Christopher Clausen has written, contrary to much that recent research has revealed about language: "By any reasonable measure, Standard English gives its users the resources for a broader range of communication, whether informational or emotional [than a dialect does]. The standard language has a larger vocabulary and more varied structures than any dialect" (24).

One might argue conversely that, because they have a passive understanding of Standard English and an active understanding of their own dialects, dialect speakers, particularly Black dialect speakers, have a broader vocabulary range and a greater variety of syntactic structures available to them, passively at least, than do speakers of so-called Network Standard. One might also quarrel with Clausen whose argument, if logically extended, would necessarily conclude, for example, that standard Arabic is inferior to Standard English because it lacks some of the constructions, such as the past conditional, that all dialects of English contain. Such an argument could also lead to the conclusion that modern Russian, Polish, and Lithuanian are superior to Standard English because these languages have a more intricate case structure for nouns and pronouns and a more highly developed system of verbal aspects than English can boast. Obviously, such an argument is not linguistically acceptable any more than Clausen's argument appears to be. Judgments like these are not valid and grow out of prejudice, gut feelings, and a misunderstanding of available linguistic data. They obscure rather than enlighten. They are elitist in nature and reveal a distressing lack of historical perspective in the view of language they present.

An unfortunate aspect of so much that has been written about the differences between Standard English and Black English is that it assumes Standard English as the model and, as such, as superior, which makes any argument that might follow specious, if not downright invalid. It seems to matter little whether the writers are white or Black; many of them make value judgments that have no place in any serious inquiry into the matter of how speakers of a dialect can best be taught the language skills, including reading, that will enable them to function adequately in their society.

Beatrice K. Levy reports on a research project she conducted with a group of 20 first grade students from the Brownsville section of New York City. All the subjects were Black, and all were from families of low socioeconomic status. Levy sought to test these children in three areas affecting language: "(1) vocabulary, (2) the mean length of T-units [thought units], and (3) three structures within T-units" (25).

Levy compared her findings with those of Roy C. O'Donnell, William J. Griffin, and Raymond G. Norris who made a similar survey of white, middle-class children of the same general age group and grade placement (26). In comparing the average T-units, she found no significant difference: the Brownsville students produced 3,449 T-units that were used in the research, and the average length was 7.03 words (27), as opposed to the 7.97 words of the white, middle-class first graders (28). Levy also discovered that the Brownsville first graders used a total number of words ranging from 631 to 3,956 (with a mean of 1,524) and that the number of different words that they used ranged from 1,187 to 533 (mean 1,336). From these data, she concluded "that none of the children can reasonably be described as nonverbal" (29).

The following conclusions in the Levy study are the most important for teachers of reading at the primary level: "The findings here indicated that, insofar as oral language knowledge is related to learning reading, the population represented by the subjects has adequate language skills. There was no evidence that the children are too deficient in linguistic abilities to learn to decode words and comprehend written communication" (30).

Every child who enters primary school does so with a well-developed background in language and linguistic structures. It is on this background that effective instruction can and must be modeled. Teachers who know how to make the most of their students' backgrounds become more aware of student abilities than of student deficits, and the learning process will thus be facilitated.

HOW DO TEACHERS FEEL ABOUT SPEAKERS OF DIALECTS?

Teachers' attitudes toward their students, particularly in the early grades, have long been considered influential in the personal and academic development of students. Recent research appears to substantiate the fact that the attitudes of teachers are all-important in instructional situations (31). Teacher attitudes of acceptance and caring toward students or toward things that students do help to promote an atmosphere conducive to learning. It is important for teachers to realize that reflecting such attitudes, especially during early learning encounters in which young children may take personally the correction of a mispronounced word or of some untoward behavior, can be crucial to the success of many young students.

It is important initially for teachers to let students know, "I like you and respect you as a person. If I seek to correct someting that you are doing, this does not change my feeling for you. I hope that you like and respect me as a person. But if I say today is Tuesday and you are sure that it is Wednesday, I want you to correct me. This will not mean that you like me or respect me any less, will it?"

Brown writes, "If the teacher is concerned only with the 'correctness' of the child's speech and not his perceptions, and attempts to force him into a system not his own (negating his system all the time), the child becomes alienated from the teacher and the culture the teacher represents" (32).

The Simons-Johnson study reaches a similar conclusion: "The authors' observations in many urban schools and their work with teachers of Black dialect speaking children suggest that the teachers' handling of dialect during reading instruction is a very important factor in Black children's poor reading performance" (33).

Teachers cannot always foresee the impact that some of their actions may have on impressionable youngsters, particularly in the very early grades. Annabel Bixby surveyed 18 adults who had been her kindergarten students 20 years earlier. Most of them spoke favorably of their kindergarten experience, devoid as it was of formality and competition for grades. However, she reports: "Many described incidents that occurred in primary grades that probably seemed trivial to their teachers but to these students seemed important. Some described times when teachers either hurt their feelings, humiliated them in front of classmates, or were unfair to them—small incidents that loomed large in their memories. *Negative experiences with teachers were mostly vividly recalled and described from their early school years, while few reported such experiences in later school life*" (34).

If learning occurs best in supportive environments, as most research indicates it does, then it is professionally incumbent upon primary teachers to provide every student with the kind of support that will motivate and enhance learning. Teachers can easily activate the "off-switch" in these early years, particularly if the child's use of language becomes the constant target of correction and, in her or his eyes, perhaps ridicule.

Teachers need to realize that just as they affect students, students affect them. All teaching involves interaction, and mature teachers will attempt to analyze their own reactions intelligently and fairly. Philip C. Schlechty and Helen E. Atwood write, "the quality and quantity of teacher interaction seem to be influenced by such factors as student sex, teacher perceptions of student achievement, and even a student's physical location in the classroom" (35). Some teachers may be unaware that factors of this kind enter into classroom interaction. Knowledge and awareness of such reactions can lead to improved teacher/student relations.

Teachers need to have a realistic view of their own tolerances or thresholds and to work at expanding these tolerances or thresholds as they mature in the profession. For example, some teachers are possessive of their space and do not like to have it intruded upon. Such teachers may make subconscious judgments about students who have a different space concept than theirs, students who like to be physically close and to touch. A judgment based on this sort of reaction is usually masked: "Johnny can't sit still" or "Susie can't seem to follow directions." Many experienced teachers cannot admit to themselves the reasons they react to some students as they do.

Labov writes: "The essential fallacy of the verbal-deprivation theory lies in tracing the educational failure of the child to his personal deficiencies. At present, these deficiencies are said to be caused by his home environment. It is traditional to explain a child's failure in school by *his* inadequacy; but when failure reaches such massive proportions, it seems necessary to look at the social and cultural obstacles to learning and the inability of the school to adjust to the social situation" (36).

Torrey addresses primary school teachers particularly when she writes: "Children in the lower grades commonly accept a teacher as a kind of substitute mother. Teachers make use of this attitude in motivating and teaching. However, no such mother-child relationship can be established with someone who cannot accept the other person and his ways as legitimate" (37). Her contentions are particularly compelling in the light of a recent research study by Barbara J. Shade that reviews the characteristic traits of Black children who are achievers. Among the generalizations this research report reaches is that "Black achievers, for the most part, come from families whose occupational level might be categorized as upper-lower class and above" (38). The study, not surprisingly in light of the findings of Labov's studies (39), "indicates that the majority of Black academic achievers are female." But most important for teachers to remember is the fact that "While it is generally noted that *there is little difference between the males and females in intelligence*, girls have been found to be identified as gifted at a 2:1 ratio" (40).

Perhaps the most surprising finding in the Shade research is that "one of the most baffling characteristics of Black achievers is their apparent ability to induce negative reactions from their teachers." Shade continues, "Although Black girls seem to obain a more favorable response from teachers than do Black males, in general Black achievers, regardless of sex, are found to be objects of rejection by teachers" (41). And then Shade specifies the bases of her conclusions: "Black gifted achievers were found to receive less attention, to be least praised, and to be most criticized in a classroom—even when compared to their nonachieving and nongifted Black counterparts" (42), which says volumes about the stereotyping of Black students by teachers—not all of whom are white.

Shade contends, "Black students respond best to teachers who are warm, interested, child-oriented, and have high expectations of students" (43). Nearly everything written about the education of Black students would support this statement. Nicholas J. Anastasiow and Michael L. Hanes, for example, write, "Our position is that the cultural variables in the poverty child's ability to learn to read are his intelligence, his ability to comprehend language as it is spoken in school, *and the teacher's acceptance of the child's dialect*" (44). The acceptance of a child's dialect and the acceptance of that child are very closely linked in the early grades—at least in the mind of the child.

In his report of 1966, James S. Coleman states that better physical facilities and better materials are not the answer to the learning problems of minority students nearly so much as good teachers are (45). What Coleman suggests calls for greater objective self-assessment and sufficient education in dialectology and in the sociology of race and culture to dispel many of the attitudinal barriers that currently affect the learning of dialect-speaking minority students.

HOW TO GET STARTED

Most teachers want to be effective. Some, however, do not know what steps to take initially to help them deal with students who are very much different from themselves. The following suggestions may help teachers who wish to deal more effectively and productively with students whose backgrounds are different from their own:

1. Learn as much as you can about the dialect(s) your students speak. [See the list of some characteristics of Black English that appears earlier in this chapter.]
2. Respect your students' dialects and their right to use them.
3. Learn to differentiate between a real error in oral reading and a translation from what is written to the dialect of the reader.
4. Respect *what* your students say and write [for what they have said or written as much as for the way it is expressed].
5. Avoid making judgments about students' intellect based largely upon *how* they express themselves.
6. Let your language be a model for your students without allowing it to be a wall which separates you from them.
7. Work to expand your students' language bases by having them listen to records or view films which represent a variety of language situations.
8. Work to expand your students' experiential bases by exposing them to the community and by bringing into the classroom local citizens from various walks of life.
9. Demonstrate to your students that you value them and are as willing to learn from them as you hope they are to learn from you. (46)

Chapter 11
THE PROS AND CONS
OF BASAL READERS

BASAL READERS DEFINED

Basal readers or, as they have recently been designated by some publishers, "reading systems" come in series by grade levels. They are sets of basic reading books, usually attractively illustrated, designed in most cases for use in grades one through eight. Sets of basal readers are accompanied by detailed teacher's manuals and by workbooks for student use. Their chief appeals are that they are sequential and that teachers with limited backgrounds in the teaching of reading can use them easily and successfully for initial instruction. Nila Banton Smith, although not blind to some of the limitations of basal readers, notes, "Vocabulary is carefully controlled from book to book, and sequential and balanced skill development programs are provided" (1).

The basal readers used in grade one are crucial because they will provide most children with their first exposure to formal reading instruction. The first grade materials will generally include a reading readiness workbook, a number of preprimers, a primer, and an initial reader, although some recent series have altered these traditional designations. At this level teachers are usually provided with other materials to use with students who are learning to read. The first half dozen stories in the first preprimer may be reproduced in the form of a large book, about two feet wide and three feet high, for use with the whole class. Pictures and cards containing letters, words, and phrases, along with a holder for such cards, are also a part of the typical basal reading package that schools buy for their first grades. Some packages have all sorts of supplementary reading materials for each level, along with such mediated materials as computer programs, filmstrips, audio cassettes, and records related to the readings and to the reinforcement of the skills stressed in the readings. Basal readers usually give their most concentrated and continuous attention to the skills of vocabulary development, word attack, and comprehension.

SOME STRENGTHS IN BASAL READERS

So entrenched has the use of basal readers been over the past half century that they must obviously be appealing to teachers and administrators, and many children using them must be demonstrating signs of success in learning to read. Even before the publication of the *Elson-Gray Readers* around 1930, a type of basal reader, the *McGuffey Readers*, had been a mainstay in American education for nearly a century. Between 1836 and 1890, a staggering 107 million copies of the *McGuffey Readers* were sold (2), and their impact on American education was great.

Wilma H. Miller applauds the eclectic approach that basal readers encourage. She also points to the organization of such readers as assets: "Although there are considerable differences between various basal reader series, the materials used in this approach do not emphasize any single reading skill at the expense of other reading skills. For example, all the word identification techniques from sight word recognition, phonic analysis, structural analysis, and contextual analysis are stressed from the initial stages of reading instruction" (3). She contends that "contemporary basal readers are now emphasizing materials from the content areas of social studies, science, and mathematics much more than was done in the past" (4).

In a recent survey, 25 teachers from grades one through five pointed to the following strengths in basal readers:

- Logical sequence of skills presented
- Easily identifiable storylines
- Variety of children's literature presented
- Increasing difficulty of stories in terms of readability
- Increasing difficulty of stories in terms of density of concepts
- Controlled vocabulary
- Convenience of having the same book for each child at a given reading level
- Presentation of comprehension and word analysis techniques. (5)

This list indicates that basal readers give teachers a sense of security and direction. It also suggests that not all teachers object to a teaching method that would seem to some people to be a lockstep method. This implication is probably not because teachers are willing to teach in a lockstep way but rather because good teachers enhance the basic materials with which they are working and thereby keep them from being lockstep.

Maryann Murphy Manning and Gary Manning say, "If basals are used in a middle school remedial reading program, they should not be followed page by page with accompanying workbooks" (6). What the Mannings suggest for middle school remedial classes is probably good advice as well for elementary school teachers who are using basal readers. Such readers can provide some excellent material for teachers, offering more variety than they can easily find in other sources, but these books should be used as the resources they are, not as textbooks to be taught from cover to cover.

SOME LIMITATIONS IN BASAL READERS

The group of teachers cited above has also identified some of the weaknesses of basal readers, and their estimations concur with those of many writers and researchers in the field:

- The story content is sometimes irrelevant to the readers' backgrounds.
- The story content is not matched to individual students' interests.
- Word analysis and comprehension skills are not fully developed.
- Too few opportunities are provided to apply word analysis and comprehension skills.
- The vocabulary is too controlled.
- Stories on current topics are insufficient.
- Individual skill needs are not met. (7)

Complaints like these are quite widespread, and Dolores Durkin, in a survey of the teacher's manuals of five basal reading series, found that perhaps part of the problem lay in the manuals themselves. Teachers will tend to stress what the manuals stress, and the lack of specific instruction on how to teach comprehension, for example, shows quite tellingly in the Durkin study: "Of the 11,587 minutes of observation [that Durkin took part in] during reading periods, only 45 minutes were spent on comprehension instruction. The 45 minutes were divided among twelve separate episodes, which means that the average length of an instance of comprehension was only 3.75 minutes" (8). Possibly the basal readers themselves are less in need of drastic revision than are the manuals that accompany them.

Durkin faults the teacher's manuals for not offering enough guidance to teachers about how to acquaint students with the vocabulary they will need in order to understand language and how it operates. Shane Templeton speaks of the *metalinguistics* of reading and identifies such words as *word*, *letter*, *sound*, and *sentence* as parts of the metalanguage that teachers will have to teach some students before fruitful work can be done in the language arts classroom (9). Templeton writes, "The language of instruction in reading *is* a metalanguage, and this explains the inability of many children to discriminate among word parts or to 'blend sounds together'—they have not yet learned the metalanguage'' (10).

Any major publishing company that offers a basal reading program has done considerable field research before embarking on an undertaking that has such significant economic implications for the company as the marketing of a basal series has. Such companies are careful to select highly knowledgeable reading specialists to compose and compile the books in the series. Because such books must be acceptable to large, diverse constituencies, they generally avoid glaring controversy and project the smiling aspects of life.

Herein lies a major weakness in such books. Often they are vapid, uninteresting, unrealistically optimistic, and, even in our time—despite efforts to reflect our society's great ethnic diversity—representative of the value system of white middle-class America. Bruno Bettelheim and Karen Zelan find that although dark-skinned children have begun to appear on the covers and in some of the pictures in basal readers, they ''all remain nameless and are not mentioned in any of the stories. It is as if in these preprimers minority children have an existence only in the background, as a foil for what goes on in the lives of the white protagonists'' (11). Efforts to bring the materials in basal readers more into the context of contemporary society have not been overwhelmingly successful, although some progress has been made.

Bettelheim and Zelan complain about the vapid selections found in most basal readers, and they also point out that these readers do not take into account sufficiently the psychology of the children who will be using them. They note that in a commonly used series, for example, the command ''Come here!'' is repeated 24 times in 177 lines of text, most of these lines being only three or four words long, and that the simpler command ''Come,'' or related statements, appears 43 times. They argue, ''Children typically hate to be told what to do, and they particularly hate the order, 'Come here!''' (12) Bettelheim and Zelan object to most readers because they condescend to children, treat them like idiots, and do not cause them to reach toward high intellectual goals.

Their conjectures are supported by the research of William Schmidt and others who have analyzed 38 basal textbooks commonly used in second, third, and fourth grades to determine their content. In the process, they segmented content into subject matter (knowing that), functional (knowing how), and ethos (knowing to)—that is, knowledge of facts, skills, and proper actions. They have found that in the 1,959 selections they reviewed, 57.7 percent have subject matter content, 29.1 percent have functional content, and 12.3 percent have ethos content. Of the selections reviewed, 4 percent have content in all three areas, and 16 percent contain content in more than one area (13).

These findings suggest that publishers of basal readers need to pay much more attention to adjusting the content of basal readers for today's youth who have developed sophisticated expectations of literature through their exposure to television and films while they are still at the prereading stage of their development.

THE LANGUAGE OF BASAL READERS

The language of most basal readers (with the exception of such highly controversial dialect readers as *Ollie*, *Friends*, and *Old Tales* produced under the direction of William A. Stewart by the Education Study Center in Washington, D.C.) is Network Standard, a dialect quite distant and distinct from that to which typical first graders in today's schools are most frequently exposed in their daily lives.

Another significant problem is that wide differences occur among the common vocabulary of basal readers. In 1960, Helen Behn examined seven commonly used preprimers and primers and reported that one-third to one-half of the vocabulary found in each was found in the others. In the same year, Walter McHugh did a similar investigation of second and third grade basal readers and found that in this group two-thirds of the vocabulary was common in all of them (14). Obviously, although the problem is not so great in the upper grades, a significant problem still existed in the primary grades when these studies were done. The implication of Behn's and McHugh's findings is that a school district has to commit itself to using one basal series in order not to place students at a disadvantage and expose them to a futile and frustrating reading experience.

Even though these studies were conducted in 1960, more recent investigations of new basal readers reach similar conclusions. Douglas P. Barnard and James DeGracie, writing in 1976, reveal that in the first grade books of the eight publishers whose reading systems they investigated, "a total of 1,778 different words [was] introduced in the new programs. At a specific level, about one-third of the words were common to two programs. When all words were considered across all levels [readiness and preprimer through first reader] only 47 percent of the words were common to two or more series" (15).

128

USING BASAL READERS IN A MOBILE SOCIETY

A related problem of considerably more importance, because it is outside the control of the school, is that of student mobility. American families are continually on the move; children who are exposed to one basal reading program in the first four or five months of first grade and who then move to a district in which another program is used, as often happens, may all at once find it difficult to read material that is thought to be at their grade level. Also, school districts may find themselves locked into a costly basal reading program. If, after three or four years of using a set, districts decide that they want to adopt another reading program, they can do so only gradually because students who have gotten two or three years into one basal program cannot be easily moved into another—nor should they be.

DIFFERENCES IN VOCABULARY FROM READER TO READER

Despite the many improvements made in the basal reading systems that appeared in the 1970s, the commonality of vocabulary is such that a child who has been exposed, for example, to the Macmillan program would have been exposed to 234 of the 510 words introduced during the first year in the Houghton-Mifflin program, or to 235 of the 675 words introduced in the first year of the Scott, Foresman program (16). Leo V. Rodenborn and Earlene Washburn, writing about six basal series they examined for vocabulary, conclude that "the variations in the vocabulary introduced in these six series indicate that it will be exceedingly difficult for children to move from one series to another during or at the end of the first grade" (17). They also express dismay—quite understandably in the light of their findings—that some school districts allow multiple adoptions of basal programs.

A LOCKSTEP APPROACH

Perhaps the most serious objection of educators to basal reading instruction is that it is a lockstep method. Most people realize that children grow at different rates, that readiness comes to them at different times, and that girls in elementary school are usually more mature than boys. Everything points to the fact that individualized instruction is the most effective type to use with beginning readers, each of whom must be encouraged to begin reading when he or she is ready to do so and each of whom must be encouraged to progress at his or her own pace, which may mean falling behind or leaping ahead of other students in the class (18). The basal reader, if it is used as directed by many teacher's manuals, requires the teacher to approach each lesson according to a specific sequence:

1. Creating interest and establishing motivation
2. Presentation and study of words new to the series
3. Reading
   a. Directed silent reading
   b. Rereading and oral reading
4. Skills development and practice
5. Follow-up (usually workbook or ditto pages). (19)

If teachers are forced to approach each selection in this manner, the pace is slow and the interest level of bright students may lag. Also, slow students for whom this approach is too fast may fall behind. The dependence on teacher direction weakness the program for students who are developing speedily. Lyman G. Hunt correctly asserts, "Until a fledgling reader is able to propel himself through printed material without teacher direction, he is not a reader" (20). Because of his belief in the validity of this statement, Hunt emphasizes the early need for more silent reading and for the sort of sustained silent reading of which mature readers must be capable. Possibly with the growing use of computer programs as supplements to basal readers, some of the problems of individualizing instruction will be overcome.

INDIVIDUALIZING INSTRUCTION

Some producers of modern basal reading systems, recognizing the need for more individualization and for more flexibility within their system, have made efforts to provide teachers with materials that will encourage a more individualized approach to reading instruction and will allow for varying rates of individual progress. One program, for example, is composed of six basic units, each of which has 50 children's books covering a broad range of interest and ability levels—biographies, scientific books, adventure books, books about fantasy, and stories about boys and girls much like those who will be reading them. Each book contains several cards, each of which directs the reader to perform certain tasks related to the book, including activities concerned with vocabulary, details, and comprehension and suggested follow-up activities. The tendency to build individualization into basal reading programs is promising, although in most cases it is still less refined at the lower grade levels than at the higher ones.

Among the more successful computer programs in reading are *Micro-Read* (21) (grades 1-8), *Pal Reading Curriculum* (22) (grades 1-6), *Reading Skills Courseware Series* (23) (grades 1-6), *Adventures of Oswald* (24) (grades K-1), *Cause and Effect* (25) (grades 2-5), *Computer Animated Reading Instruction System* (26) (grades K-1), *Context Clues* (27) (grades 2-5), *Drawing Conclusions* (28) (grades 2-5), *Inference* (29) (grades 2-5), *Letter Recognition* (30) (grades K-1), *Magic Wand Books* (31) (grades 1-4), *Reading Is Fun* (32) (grades 3-6), and *Story Machine* (33) (grades 1-3). These programs provide the kind of individualization of instruction that teachers have long been seeking.

INCREASED VOCABULARY

One promising aspect of some new basal programs is that they are introducing students to more extensive vocabularies, as well as to more sophisticated grammatical structures, than were found in earlier series. The latter phenomenon may be attributable to the fact that in the last two decades, numerous highly competent linguists have turned their attention to reading instruction. Arthur V. Olson's analysis in 1965 of the vocabulary used in seven basal reading series at the primary level revealed that the average number of words introduced to students during their first year of reading instruction was 324 (34). Barnard and DeGracie, doing a comparable study 10 years later, found that the average number of new words introduced in eight of the new basal reading systems was 504 (35). For whatever reason, there has been a 66-percent increase in the number of words taught.

George D. Spache and Evelyn B. Spache reported in 1969 that of the basal readers then in common use, the cumulative vocabulary at the end of the first reader ranged, according to the program, from 230 to 475 words (36). The comparative study of six new basal readers that Rodenborn and Washburn did in 1974 (37) revealed increases in the cumulative vocabulary at the end of the first year at the lower end of the scale: the program that introduced the smallest number of new words (324) introduced almost 50 percent more words than the comparable book in the Spaches' investigation. But more significant is the fact that while the largest cumulative vocabulary noted in the Spaches' study was 475, the comparable figure in the Rodenborn-Washburn study was 675.

The Barnard-DeGracie study, published in 1976, examined eight major basal programs and presented even more encouraging data than did the Rodenborn-Washburn study. Barnard and DeGracie found that the cumulative number of words introduced by the end of the first reader ranged from a low of 440 to a high of 811, with the next highest program they analyzed introducing 614 words (38).

The implications of this percentage gain are in themselves important. The broader the vocabulary range of initial reading materials, the more varied they can be and the more grammatically sophisticated they can become. However, another interesting finding in the Rodenborn-Washburn report is that 51 of the 298 common words found in the six basal readers examined are not found on the Harris-Jacobson List for First Grade (39), certainly suggesting that a broader range of relevant material is being presented in the new basal readers than was apparent in their predecessors.

ARE BASAL READERS RELEVANT FOR TODAY'S STUDENTS?

Basal readers have been attacked through the years for their irrelevance to the lives of students. Fred Busch writes: "The bland, pollyanna-ish content found in most first grade reading texts not only stifles the growth process, but more importantly may communicate to the child that this [the growth process] must be something to be frightened of and avoided. Why else would the characters not show emotion that is negative as well as positive, feel anxiety and pain, or experience conflicts?" (40). The problem Busch addresses here is a highly complex one, and it has not yet been overcome completely. However, the broadening of the vocabulary used in the first grade readers is a promising sign. Also, one cannot deny the validity of Terry Johnson's statement: "The last few years have seen a marked improvement in reading programmes with regard to content. More readers deal with city children, colored children, and children with problems." Johnson complains, though, that "literary merit is still lacking in the earliest readers" (41), and one might also add that it is in the earlier readers that the material is still the most unrealistic and vapid.

Change does not come quickly, particularly to anything as large as a reading program. Publishers who gamble extravagantly risk losing huge sums of money and seriously jeopardizing the economic futures of their companies if they go too far afield in the basal series. Nevertheless, a sensitivity to social change is beginning to show itself in some areas of textbook publishing.

GENDER BIAS IN BASAL READERS

Thomas R. Schnell and Judith Sweeney have conducted a limited study on sex role bias in basal readers and have reached some disturbing conclusions. In comparing the 1966 and 1971 editions of just one major basal reading program, they found that stories featuring boys had increased from 39.4 percent in 1966 to 51.2 percent in 1971, while stories featuring girls had dropped from 15.8 percent to 12.5 percent in the same period. They also found that illustrations showing boys had increased from 56.2 percent to 70.5 percent, while illustrations showing girls had dropped from 43.8 percent to 29.5 percent. All the statistics they cite indicate that women received less representation in the 1971 edition than in the earlier edition, and particularly that the imbalance was greater in the first grade than in other grades. It must be pointed out, however, that they examined just one series, albeit a frequently used one (42)—and that similar studies should be made on a broader scale.

Another pertinent study in this area is that of Lenore J. Weitzman and Diane Rizzo (43). In 1974 they analyzed illustrations found in textbooks used in average United States classrooms in grades one through six over a five-year period for their latent content about male and female behavior. Among their findings were the following:

- Females made up only 31 percent of the total illustrations, males 69 percent. The percentage of illustrations showing females decreased from lower grades to higher grades, whereas the percentage of illustrations showing males increased.
- A strong contrast was found between the activities of boys and girls. Boys were involved in action and adventure, in outdoor pursuits; girls were found to be passive and indoors.
- Differences in emotional expresson were noted. Girls were shown expressing a wider range of emotions than boys, who were shown controlling emotions—being strong and silent.
- In the reading series, among all the story titles, boys were predominant in 102 stories; girls were featured in 35 stories in which they reinforced traditional female roles. Females predominated in two areas—as mean and evil characters (witches and villains) and as clumsy or stupid people or objects of jokes.

Gender bias in basal readers seems to be moderating somewhat. Nevertheless, in a recent survey of how reading was depicted in five basal series, grades one through eight, Jackie L. Green-Wilder and Albert J. Kingston found that 123 males were depicted as readers whereas 101 females were (44). Clearly, the latent content of many textbooks deserves further serious consideration.

THE DEPICTION OF THE ELDERLY IN BASAL READERS

The 1980 census showed that 11.4 percent of all Americans are over 65 years of age. Despite the greying of America, many children do not know any older people well. In many cases, their grandparents are still under 65 and are still working. Also, with the mobility of Americans, many live at substantial distances from older relatives and see them infrequently.

Literature provides young students, 80 to 95 percent of whom use basal readers, with a means of coming to know something about older people and to understand them. However, students whose chief reading is done in basal readers will have little opportunity to meet the elderly in the pages of these books. A recent review by Judith K. Serra and Pose Lamb of four basal series, grades one through six, reveals that 6.8 percent of the 1,036 stories reviewed included elderly people (45).

The researchers identified six basic categories in which the elderly were depicted in the readers they examined: "Children having a relationship with an elderly relative; elderly seen as wise and inspirational; elderly facing hurt, problems, or challenges; elderly having a close relationship with an unrelated person; elderly seen as socially active; elderly seen as breaking male or female stereotypes" (46). Serra and Lamb agree that "some progress [has been made] in the areas of stories dealing with sickness, problems, and challenges of the aged, close relationships with non-related elderly, and breaking 'old' stereotypes" (47), but they call for more stories that deal with elderly people who are socially active, who break male/female stereotypes, and who deal with death more deeply than do the elderly in most of the selections they reviewed.

Basically, however, the great need is simply for more selections that include the elderly. Serra and Lamb found a shockingly small number of selections that included them, and for the purposes of their study, they included every selection that even mentioned an older person.

DEALING WITH BIAS IN BASAL READERS

Students cannot be protected from bias—nor should they be. Rather they should be trained to recognize, analyze, and deal with bias, be it in basal readers or in television shows or in advertising. Sara Goodman Zimet has suggested specific ways in which teachers can help young students to recognize bias within the materials they read.

She suggests that teachers have a questionnaire to give their students that will be usable with every selection they read. It might ask such questions as these: "Is there a character who looks like me in this story?" "Does anyone in the story have hair like mine?" "Is anyone in the story about my age?" "Is anyone in the story as tall (fat, short, thin) as I am?" "Does anyone in the story have parents who do the kinds of work my mother and father do?" Using the questionnaire with a multiracial group of physically handicapped children, one teacher then set her class to work trying to find stories that contained characters more like themselves than the stories in the basal reader.

She also tried to get students to understand some of their own biases by asking them to put at the top of a column the words "Black/dark" and then to write beneath them any words they associated with these two words. She did the same with "White/fair," "Fat," and "Thin." Her students were amazed to see the kinds of associations they made—usually associating "black" with negative feelings and "white" with positive ones, "fat" with comic feelings and "thin" with both attractiveness and meanness.

As a follow-up, she had her students associate the words they had worked with with stories they had read (48). This procedure, used with children as early as the first two primary grades, can help youngsters to build good reading habits as well as strong reasoning powers.

THE STUDENTS' READING NEEDS

Child psychologists have written voluminously to counter the notion that young children will be adversely affected by an introduction to literature that deals with problems like those they face in their own lives. Erik Erikson has written of children's need during the latency stage to find a means of dealing with what is going on inside them (49). Their early literary experiences could meet this need except for the fact that parents have not yet been made fully aware of the desirability of exposing children to the sort of searching questions that might be evoked. Until a campaign to educate the public succeeds, it is doubtful that change in basal readers will be as pronounced as informed educators and psychologists would like it to be.

Chapter 12
READING'S PAST AND FUTURE

The present of reading is so much with us that it is easy to forget its past and to ignore its future. The ascendancy of reading in the western world began when Johann Gutenberg invented a printing press using movable type, probably in Strasbourg in either 1436 or 1437. It took some two decades before Gutenberg's first book came from this press, the exquisite Mazarin Bible, also known as the Gutenberg Bible, the publication date of which is thought to be 1456.

Gutenberg did not experience instant fame and fortune as a result of his first major publication. Indeed, Johann Fust, a goldsmith from whom Gutenberg had borrowed the money to set up his press and produce his Bible, foreclosed on the mortgage when the printer was unable to repay his loan. The press thus fell into the hands of Fust and his son-in-law, Peter Schoffer, who continued to operate it.

It was not until 1471 or 1472 that William Caxton learned in Cologne the art of printing with movable type. In Bruges in 1475, with the help of Colard Mansion, Caxton printed *The Recuyell of the Historyes of Troye*, the first book ever to be printed in English. The following year Caxton set up a press near Westminster which, before the turn of the century, had produced editions of approximately 100 titles.

This is not to suggest that suddenly reading became a favorite pastime of the British peasantry. Indeed, few people in European or British society were able to read; books were therefore produced largely for the educated few—mostly clergymen—who were literate.

It was not until the Reformation, which began some 60 years after the publication of the Mazarin Bible, that Martin Luther espoused the doctrine that every person should learn to read sufficiently well to be able to read Scripture, thereby making every person an interpreter of Holy Writ.

Gutenberg and Luther served as instrumentalities in the movement toward universal literacy in the western world. One provided the physical means of producing books in multiple copies; the other provided a philosophical basis for encouraging the masses to learn how to read. Two major stumbling blocks to universal literacy were overcome in less than a century—nevertheless literacy did not begin to sweep Europe or Britain as a result.

Shakespeare and Marlowe and Kyd were writing during this period, but they were not writing to be read. Rather, they were writing to be performed and their audiences were largely illiterate. Indeed, playwrights of the day went to extraordinary lengths to see that written versions of their plays did not leave the theatre after rehearsals because they feared that their material would be pirated were it to get ito the wrong hands. Popular literature remained essentially part of the oral tradition which developed in the story-telling and history-preserving traditions of ancient peoples throughout the world. Literature that was intended to be read remained essentially a literature produced by clerics for a clerical audience. Other literate members of this society included some merchants who had sufficient reading and writing abilities to enable them to keep records of their transactions, even as the tradespeople of ancient Sumeria, Babylonia, and Egypt had before them.

Neil Postman, addressing the impact of increased possibilities for communication, writes: "Technological changes in our modes of communication are even more ideology-laden than changes in our modes of transportation. Introduce the alphabet to a culture and you change its cognitive habits, its social relations, its notions of community, history and religion." He goes on: "Introduce the printing press with movable type, and you do the same. Introduce speed-of-light transmission of images and you make a cultural revolution. Without a vote. Without polemics. Without guerrilla resistance" (1). Ideas are humankind's most potent weapons, and it is in written form that ideas are most reliably preserved.

The historical purposes of writing are essentially fourfold: (1) it preserves tradition, (2) it allows expression, (3) it records information, and (4) it makes possible the dissemination of that information. The ancient drawings in the caves at Altamira and Lascaux, the carefully wrought Coptic inscriptions found in the Egyptian pyramids, the cuneiform wedges found on ancient tablets of clay, the graffiti found on the sides of Pompeian buildings or on the walls of the New York subway system—all these examples of writing and recording serve such purposes.

As long as society was essentially agrarian, there was little need for the average person to be able to read. An economy based largely on the exchange of products is a much less abstract economy than one that is based, to a large extent, on the exchange of information. When the exchange of products is a simple one-to-one exchange, such as one person's trading a sheep he has raised for a garment fashioned by a neighbor, no written records need enter into the transfer.

When entrepreneurs are involved, as they necessarily are if exchanges take place among people too separated from each other geographically to deal on a one-to-one basis, written records become a necessity, and some form of literacy becomes a requirement for the entrepreneurs. When an economy comes to be based on services as much as or more than on the production of goods, as is the case with modern economy, then literacy is a requirement for anyone who wishes to participate fully in that economy and in the society it serves.

It was the coming of the Industrial Age that marked a turning point in the importance of reading. When an industrialized society becomes sufficiently complex to demand that information must be systematically created and preserved, such a society requires continually higher levels of education for its members, making it incumbent upon them to know how to read in order to have available to them the information they are required to master.

If we view reading as part of a continuum stretching back to the earliest human history on earth, we find that it does not soon appear on that continuum in any way. Humans and humanlike creatures used language in systematic forms for eons before they developed systems of writing; and even then they wrote pictographically so that communication was through pictures rather than through abstract symbols.

The move from pictographic representation to ideographic representation was an incomprehensibly enormous advance for the species to make because it took humankind to a totally new level of abstract representation. And the leap from ideographic writing to alphabetic writing probably represents an advance more significant and more incredible than that of putting the first humans on the moon.

Edward T. Hall speaks of the development of writing and, by extension, of its concomitant, reading: "The history of art is almost three times longer than that of writing, and the relationship between the two types of expression can be seen in the earliest forms of writing, such as the Egyptian hieroglyphics. However, very few people treat art as a system of communication which is historically linked with language" (2).

The oldest written records left by humankind are drawings etched on the walls of caves or carved on the organic materials from which their simple tools were made. At the time such graphic representations were made, everyone within that culture could read them; that is, they could look at them and know what they meant. The level of abstraction required in order for a person to read them was much lower than the level of abstraction required of one who is trying to learn to read an alphabetic language today, and teachers must understand this difference. Getting messages from pictures in a book *is* a form of reading, and most people can handle such reading. Indeed, on our time continuum, the first very small dot represents just such reading. The dot grows slightly larger as pictographic and alphabetic writing develop, but it is still so small as to be almost imperceptible. And it remains imperceptibly small until the invention of the printing press and the urgings toward literacy of Martin Luther.

Only in the present century has reading begun to appear on the continuum as a large circle rather than as a dot. Its appearance as a large circle has coincided with the enormous growth on the one hand, of industry and, on the other hand, of free public education, made available through legal mandate in most developed areas of the world and imposed on young people through compulsory attendance laws in most civilized places. Because this is the current situation, many people forget the past and fail to recognize that in the future the continuum may place reading in a much less important position, relatively speaking, than it enjoys today.

This is not to suggest that reading will fall into a position of unimportance or that human beings in the future will not have to be able to read. Reading is firmly entrenched as a requisite skill that members of complex societies must possess. However, other means of communication, many of them invented or refined and made readily available to millions of people within the past century, may drastically alter the purposes to which people turn their reading skills.

In addition, significant strides are being made in reading instruction. For example, one of the most promising systems that has been developed is tightly organized and highly sequential; it aims to teach the skills of literacy—reading and writing—as early and as quickly as possible. Although it is still early to generalize on the results of a system such as this, it is encouraging to find that some school districts that have employed it have eliminated illiteracy in all students by fifth grade.

As teaching systems of this sort are developed, universal literacy may be achieved. There will one day be no illiterates in developed nations, and other elements of communications systems will occupy a more important position on the continuum than reading does. Such areas as subliminal communication, which is already being studied seriously by a number of eminent scholars and researchers, may be developed in ways that will enable people to communicate by means that seem unavailable to them today.

For the present, initial reading instruction is vital and necessary. It is most likely to be successful if those teaching it are not overburdened with large classes and if they have accurate current knowledge of scientific developments in the broad area of human communication. In most cases this means that school districts should be spending much more money than they are now on staffing the primary grades, on providing materials for those grades, and on providing teachers at the primary level with ample opportunity to continue their education so that they can remain current in their teaching techniques. Money spent in this way will substantially reduce expenditures for later remedial instruction in reading which, for the most part, is offered too late to do much good.

But broader benefits will accrue to society if all children learn to read in the primary grades—and this *can* happen. Of greatest importance is the fact that in developed societies, literate people have a greater sense of their own worth than those who are not literate do. On the most crass level, literate people contribute more to society in tax revenues than illiterates do. Their other contributions generally are also such that society benefits from their ability to exercise their literacy.

It is necessary to realize that, for better or worse, civilization is moving conceptually at a breakneck speed. Writing of the past, Alvin Toffler states: "In stagnant societies, the past crept forward into the present and repeated itself in the future. In such a society, the most sensible way to prepare a child was to arm him with the skills of the past—for these were precisely the same skills he would need in the future" (3). To a large extent, this was the form that education took until the beginning of this century. Future orientation is a relatively new phenomenon. Although Toffler recognizes that such basics as reading and writing and mathematics will be necessary to people who wish to function well in the society of the future, he cautions his readers that "millions of children today are forced by law to spend precious hours of their lives grinding away at materials whose future utility is highly questionable" (4). His most telling message for reading teachers is that "Tomorrow's illiterate will not be the man who can't read; he will be the man who has not learned how to learn" (5).

What Toffler really means is that reading is an instrumentality. Being able to read does not *make* a person smart or productive or successful. Rather, being able to read makes it more possible for a person to function intelligently and effectively within modern society. This is the perspective that reading teachers most need to develop.

NOTES

Chapter 1. A Look at Reading Instruction, pp. 5-13.

1. Jeanne Chall, *Learning to Read: The Great Debate* (New York: McGraw-Hill, 1976).
2. Nila Banton Smith, *Why Do the Schools Teach Reading as They Do?* (Lake Forest, IL: National School Public Relations Association, 1955), 5.
3. Neil Postman, *Amusing Ourselves to Death: Public Discourse in the Age of Show Business* (New York: Viking, 1985), 61-62.
4. Bruno Bettelheim and Karen Zelan, *On Learning to Read: The Child's Fascination with Meaning* (New York: Alfred A. Knopf, 1982), 13.
5. *Ibid.*, 21.
6. *Ibid.*, 27.
7. Wilma H. Miller, *Teaching Elementary Reading Today* (New York: Holt, Rinehart and Winston, 1984), 4-8.
8. See, for example, George W. McConkie and David Zola, "Eye Movement Techniques in Studying Differences Among Developing Readers," in *Biobehavioral Measures of Dyslexia*, edited by D. Grey and J. Kavanagh (Parkton, MD: York Press, 1986).
9. Leonard Bloomfield, *Language*, (New York: Holt, 1933).
10. Leonard Bloomfield, "Linguistics and Reading," *Elementary English Review* 19 (April and May 1942): 125-30, 183-86.
11. Clarence L. Barnhart, "The Story of the Bloomfield System," in *Let's Read: A Linguistic Approach*, edited by Leonard Bloomfield and Clarence L. Barnhart (Detroit: Wayne State University Press, 1961), 9.
12. *Ibid.* In this respect, Bloomfield's suggestions are quite similar to those that Bettelheim and Zelan make.
13. Leonard Bloomfield, "Teaching Children to Read," in Bloomfield and Barnhart, *Let's Read*, 26.
14. Charles C. Fries, *Linguistics and Reading* (New York: Holt, Rinehart, and Winston, 1963), 131.
15. *Ibid.*, 130. Fries's italics.
16. *Ibid.*, 131. Italics added.
17. *Ibid.*, xvii.
18. George A. Miller, "Some Preliminaries to Psycholinguistics," *American Psychologist* 20 (1965): 18.
19. Miles A. Tinker and Constance M. McCullough, *Teaching Elementary Reading*, 2d ed. (New York: Appleton-Century-Crofts, 1962), 378.
20. William S. Gray, *The Teaching of Reading and Writing* (Paris: UNESCO, 1956), 68.

21. Jeanne Chall and Allan F. Mirsky, eds., *Education and the Brain*, 77th Yearbook of the National Society for the Study of Education, Part II (Chicago: The Society, 1978).
22. Robert E. Ornstein, *The Psychology of Consciousness* (San Francisco: W. H. Freeman, 1972).
23. Robert E. Ornstein, *The Nature of Human Consciousness* (San Francisco: W. H. Freeman, 1973).
24. Jerome S. Bruner, *The Process of Education* (Cambridge, MA: Harvard University Press, 1960).
25. Robert Samples and Robert Wohlford, *Opening* (Reading, MA: Addison-Wesley, 1974).
26. Robert Persig, *Zen and the Art of Motorcycle Maintenance* (New York: Wiliam Morrow, 1974).
27. Robert Samples, *The Metaphoric Mind* (Reading, MA: Addison-Wesley, 1976).
28. Denny T. Wolfe, Jr., "Reading and the Brain," in *English Teaching and the Brain*, edited by Denny T. Wolfe, Jr. (San Diego: Coronado Publishers, 1986).

Chapter 2. Pathways to Reading, pp. 14-23.

1. Charlotte Cox, "Learning to Read, Reading to Learn: An Interview with Jeanne S. Chall," *Curriculum Review* 22 (December 1983): 11-15.
2. Keith Topping, "An Introduction to Paired Reading," in *Parental Involvement in Children's Reading*, edited by Keith Topping and Sheila Wolfendale (New York: Nichols, 1985), 109.
3. Jerry L. Johns, "First Graders' Concepts about Print," *Reading Research Quarterly* 15 (1980): 529.
4. Bruno Bettelheim and Karen Zelan, *On Learning to Read: The Child's Fascination with Meaning* (New York: Alfred A. Knopf, 1982), 22.
5. Gary Manning and Maryann M. Manning, "Early Readers and Nonreaders from Low Socioeconomic Environments: What Their Parents Report," *The Reading Teacher* 38 (October 1984): 34.
6. P. David Pearson and Rand J. Spiro, "Toward a Theory of Reading Comprehension," *Topics in Language Disorders* 1 (December 1980): 71-88.
7. Karen K. Wixson, "Questions About a Text: What You Ask Is What Children Learn," *The Reading Teacher* 37 (December 1983): 292.
8. *Ibid.*, 287.
9. Yetta Goodman and Bess Altwerger, *Print Awareness in Pre-School Children: A Working Paper* (Tucson: Arizona Center for Research and Development, September 1981).
10. Shelley B. Wepner, "Linking Logos with Print for Beginning Reading Success," *The Reading Teacher* 38 (March 1985): 633-39.

11. Marilyn Goodall, "Can Four Year Olds 'Read' Words in the Environment?" *The Reading Teacher* 37 (February 1984): 478-82.
12. Bettelheim and Zelan, *On Learning to Read*, 163-64.
13. Lea M. McGee, "Awareness of Text Structure: Effects on Children's Recall of Expository Text," *Reading Research Quarterly* 17 (1982): 581.
14. See Gordon Bower, "Experiments in Story Understanding and Recall," *Quarterly Journal of Experimental Psychology* 28 (November 1976): 511-34; and Jean Mandler and Nancy Johnson, "Remembrance of Things Parsed: Story Structure and Recall," *Cognitive Psychology* 9 (January 1977): 111-51.
15. Lesley Mandel Morrow, "Reading and Retelling Stories: Strategies for Emergent Readers," *The Reading Teacher* 38 (May 1985): 870.
16. Carol Lauritzen, "Oral Literature and the Teaching of Reading," *The Reading Teacher* 33 (April 1980): 787-90.
17. *Ibid.*, 789.
18. Miriam Martinez and Nancy Roser, "Read It Again: The Value of Repeated Readings During Storytime," *Reading Teacher* 38 (April 1985): 782-86.
19. As reported by Pat Cunningham, "Curriculum Trends in Reading," *Educational Leadership* 41 (April 1984): 83.

Chapter 3. How Young Children Learn, pp. 24-35.

1. See Chapter 4 for more information on reading readiness.
2. Frances L. Ilg, "The Child from Three to Eight with Implications for Reading," Address presented at a conference on Teaching the Young Child to Read, November 14-16, 1962, in Washington, DC, and reproduced in some detail in Nila Banton Smith, *Reading Instruction for Today's Children* (Englewood Cliffs, NJ: Prentice-Hall, 1963), 26.
3. *Ibid.*, 27. Ilg's italics.
4. *Ibid*.
5. Herman T. Epstein, "Growth Spurts During Brain Development: Implications for Educational Policy and Practice," in *Education and the Brain*, edited by Jeanne Chall and Allan F. Mirsky, 77th Yearbook of the National Society for the Study of Education, Part II (Chicago: The Society, 1978), 344.
6. R. S. Hampleman, "A Study of the Comparative Reading Achievement of Early and Late School Starters," *Elementary English* 34 (1959): 331-34.
7. L. B. Carter, "The Effect of Early School Entrance on the Scholastic Achievement of Elementary School Children in the Austin Public Schools," *Journal of Educational Research* 50 (1956): 91-113.
8. Albert J. Harris, *How to Increase Your Reading Ability*, 4th ed. (New York: Longmans, Green, 1961).

9. E. L. Thorndike, *The Psychology of Learning* (New York: Teachers College, Columbia University, 1923).

10. Arnold Gesell, *The Mental Growth of the Pre-School Child* (New York: Macmillan, 1925). See also his later books *Infancy and Human Growth* (New York: Macmillan, 1928) and *The First Five Years of Life* (New York: Harper and Brothers, 1940).

11. See Dolores Durkin, "Children Who Read Before Grade One," *The Reading Teacher* 14 (1961): 163-66. See also her *Children Who Read Early* (New York: Teachers College Press, Columbia University, 1966).

12. See George W. McConkie and David Zola, "Eye Movement Techniques in Studying Differences Among Developing Readers," in *Biobehavioral Measures of Dyslexia*, edited by D. Gray and J. Kavanaugh (Parkton, MD: York Press, 1986); and N. Roderick Underwood and David Zola, "The Span of Letter Recognition of Good and Poor Readers," *Reading Research Quarterly* 21 (1986): 6-19.

13. Jerome S. Bruner, *The Process of Education* (Cambridge, MA: Harvard University Press, 1960).

14. Lawrence Kohlberg, "Early Education: A Cognitive-Development View," Unpublished paper, University of Chicago, no date, cited in Dolores Durkin, "When Should Children Begin to Read?" in *Innovation and Change in Reading Instruction*, edited by Helen M. Robinson, 67th Yearbook of the National Society for the Study of Education, Part II (Chicago: The Society, 1968), 67.

15. Jeanne Chall and Allan F. Mirsky, "The Implications of Education," in *Chall and Mirsky, Education and the Brain*, 371.

16. Robert M. Gagné, "Some New Ways of Learning and Instruction," *Phi Delta Kappan* 51 (1970): 469.

17. See particularly Bruner's *The Process of Education* and also his *On Knowing: Essays for the Left Hand* (New York: Atheneum, 1966).

18. See *Taxonomy of Educational Objectives, Handbook I* (New York: David McKay, 1956), which Bloom edited.

19. David H. Russell, "Research on the Processes of Thinking with Some Applications to Reading," *Elementary English* 42 (1965): 378.

20. Jean Piaget and Barbel Inhelder, *The Psychology of the Child* (New York: Basic Books, 1969), 6.

21. Madeline Hunter, "The Learning Process," in *The Teacher's Handbook*, edited by Dwight Allen and Eli Seifman (Glenview, IL: Scott, Foresman, 1971), 158. Hunter's italics are omitted.

22. *Ibid.*, 159. Hunter's italics omitted.

23. *Ibid.*, 160.

24. Albert North Whitehead, "The Rhythm of Education," in *The Aims of Education* (New York: Macmillan, 1959). This essay was first published as a a pamphlet (London: Christopher's, 1922).

25. *Ibid.*, 25.

26. *Ibid.*, 26.
27. See particularly Bruno Bettelheim and Karen Zelan, *On Learning to Read: The Child's Fascination with Meaning* (New York: Alfred A. Knopf, 1982), 7-23, *passim*; and Charlotte Cox, "Learning to Read, Reading to Learn: An Interview with Jeanne S. Chall," *Curriculum Review* 22 (December 1983): 11-15.
28. Whitehead, "The Rhythm of Education," 27.
29. Epstein, "Growth Spurts," 343.
30. *Ibid.*, 343-44. Epstein's italics.
31. *Ibid.*, 350.
32. *Ibid.*, 344.
33. Kohlberg, "Early Education," 67.
34. For a clear beginning discussion of hemisphericity, see Betty Jane Wagner, "Educational Drama and the Brain's Right Hemisphere," in *Educational Drama for Today's Schools*, edited by R. Baird Shuman (Metuchen, NJ: Scarecrow Press, 1978), 133-54. Jerome S. Bruner's *On Knowing: Essays for the Left Hand* is concerned with the topic as well. Also of interest is Bob Samples, *The Metaphoric Mind* (Reading, MA: Addison-Wesley, 1976). A more specialized book is Robert E. Ornstein, *The Psychology of Consciousness* (New York: Viking, 1972). Also of interest is *English Teaching and the Brain*, edited by Denny T. Wolfe, Jr. (San Diego: Coronado Publishers, 1986), which has a chapter on reading and the brain.
35. As reported in Merlin C. Wittrock, "Education and the Cognitive Processes of the Brain," in Chall and Mirsky, *Education and the Brain*, 66-67.
36. *Ibid.*, 74.
37. Wittrock cites numerous studies, among them Michael R. Raugh and Richard C. Atkinson, "A Mnemonic Method for Learning a Second-Language Vocabulary," *Journal of Educational Psychology* 67 (1975): 1-16; Joel R. Levin, "What Have We Learned About Maximizing What Children Learn?" in *Cognitive Learning in Children: Theories and Strategies*, edited by Joel R. Levin and Vernon L. Allen (New York: Academic Press, 1976), 105-34; and William D. Rohwer, Jr., "Images and Pictures in Children's Learning: Research Results and Instructional Implications," *Psychological Bulletin* 73 (1970): 393-403.
38. Wittrock, "Education and the Cognitive Processes," 97. The study to which he refers is Carolyn B. Marks, Marleen J. Doctorow, and Merlin C. Wittrock, "Word Frequency and Reading Comprehension," *Journal of Educational Research* 67 (1974): 259-62.

Chapter 4. When Are Children Ready to Read? pp. 36-47.

1. Ethelouise Carpenter, "Readiness Is Being," *Childhood Education* 38 (1961): 116.

2. J. Estill Alexander and others, eds., *Teaching Reading* (Boston: Little, Brown, 1983), 28.
3. N. Roderick Underwood and David Zola, "The Span of Letter Recognition of Good and Poor Readers," *Reading Research Quarterly* 21 (1986): 6-19. See also Jean Turner Goins, *Visual Perception Abilities and Early Reading Progress*, Supplementary Educational Monographs, 87 (Chicago: University of Chicago Press, 1958); and George W. McConkie and David Zola, "Eye Movement Techniques in Studying Differences Among Developing Readers," in *Biobehavioral Measures of Dyslexia*, edited by D. Gray and J. Kavanagh (Parkton, MD: York Press, 1986).
4. David P. Ausubel, *The Psychology of Meaningful Verbal Learning* (New York: Grune and Stratton, 1963), 33.
5. Albert J. Harris, "Child Development and Reading," in *Reading Instruction: An International Forum*, edited by Marion D. Jenkinson (Newark, DE: International Reading Association, 1967), 336-49, *passim*.
6. Ausubel, *Psychology*, 111.
7. *Ibid*.
8. Patricia Cunningham and others, *Reading in Elementary Classrooms* (New York: Longman, 1983).
9. Shane Templeton, "Literacy, Readiness, and Basals," *The Reading Teacher* 39 (1986): 403-409.
10. Dolores Durkin, "Teachers' Manuals in Basal Reading Programs," in *Reading Education: Foundations for a Literate America*, edited by Jean Osborn, Paul T. Wilson, and Richard C. Anderson (Lexington, MA: Lexington Books, 1985), 5.
11. Jackie L. Green-Wilder and Albert J. Kingston, "The Depiction of Reading in Five Popular Basal Series," *The Reading Teacher* 39 (1986): 399-402.
12. Edward W. Dolch, *Teaching Primary Reading*, 3d ed. (Champaign, IL: Garrard Press, 1960), 45-66, *passim*.
13. Dolores Durkin, "What Does Research Say About the Time to Begin Reading Instruction?" *Journal of Educational Research* 64 (October 1952): 52.
14. *Ibid*.
15. Ausubel, *Psychology*, 32.
16. Miles A. Tinker and Constance M. McCullough, *Teaching Elementary Reading*, 2d ed. (New York: Appleton-Century-Crofts, 1962), 54.
17. Michael A. Wallach and Lise Wallach, *Teaching All Children to Read* (Chicago: University of Chicago Press, 1976), 72.
18. Dolores Durkin, "An Early Start in Reading?" *Elementary School Journal* 43 (December 1962): 151.
19. McConkie and Zola, "Eye Movement Techniques."
20. M. Lucile Harrison, *Reading Readiness* (Boston: Houghton Mifflin, 1936).
21. Arthur I. Gates, G. L. Bond, and D. H. Russell, *Methods of Determining Reading Readiness* (New York: Bureau of Publications, Teachers College, Columbia University, 1939).

22. Mabel V. Morphett and Carleton Washburne, "When Should Children Begin to Read?" *Elementary School Journal* 31 (1931): 496-508.
23. Robert Rosenthal and Lenore Jacobson, *Pygmalion in the Classroom: Teacher Expectation and Pupils' Intellectual Development* (New York: Holt, Rinehart and Winston, 1968). See also R. Rosenthal, "Self-Fulfilling Prophecies in the Classroom: Teachers' Expectations as Unintended Determinants of Pupils' Intellectual Competence," in *Social Class, Race, and Psychological Development*, edited by M. Deutsch, I. Katz, and A. R. Jensen (New York: Holt, Rinehart and Winston, 1968).
24. Meredyth Daneman and Adèle Blennerhassett, "How to Assess the Listening Comprehension Skills of Prereaders," *Journal of Educational Psychology* 76 (1984): 1379.
25. *Ibid.*, 1375.
26. *Ibid.*, 1380.
27. Durkin, "What Does Research Say," 56.
28. Templeton, "Literacy, Readiness, and Basals," 407.
29. Sandra Stotsky, "Research on Reading/Writing Relationships: A Synthesis and Suggested Directions," *Language Arts* 60 (1983): 627.
30. John Downing and Renate Valtin, eds., *Language Awareness and Learning to Read* (New York: Springer Verlag, 1984).
31. Maryann Murphy Manning and Gary L. Manning, *Improving Spelling in the Middle Grades* (Washington, DC: National Education Association, 1981), 9.
32. Templeton, "Literacy, Readiness, and Basals," 407.
33. S. Hurska, "Namewriting: A Step Toward Writing and Reading," *Day Care Early Education* 12 (Winter 1984): 36-38.
34. Donald D. Durrell, "Letter-Name Values in Reading and Spelling," *Reading Research Quarterly* 16 (1980): 160.
35. Jack A. Holmes, "What Should and Could Johnny Learn to Read?" in *Challenge and Experiment in Reading*, edited by J. Allen Figurel (Newark, DE: International Reading Association, 1962), 240-41.
36. F. L. Ilg and L. B. Ames, *School Readiness: Behavior Tests Used at Gesell Institute* (New York: Harper and Row, 1965).
37. Jeannette Jansky and Katrina de Hirsch, *Preventing Reading Failure: Prediction, Diagnosis, Intervention* (New York: Harper and Row, 1972), 4.
38. The citation is to J. M. Tanner, *Education and Physical Growth* (London: University of London Press, 1961).
39. Albert J. Harris, "Evaluating Reading Readiness Tests," in *Problem Areas in Reading—Some Observations and Recommendations*, edited by Coleman Morrison, Rhode Island College Reading Conference Proceedings (Providence, RI: Oxford Press, 1965), 11-12.
40. Clarence S. Darrow, *Farmington* (Chicago: A. C. McClurg, 1904), 40-41.
41. Norbert Weiner, *Ex-Prodigy* (Cambridge: Massachusetts Institute of Technology Press, 1964), 62.

42. Durkin, "An Early Start," 151.
43. George D. Spache and others, *A Study of a Longitudinal First-Grade Readiness Program*, Cooperative Research Project No. 2742 (Tallahassee: Florida State Department of Education, 1965).
44. Excellent suggestions for creating reading and experiential situations in classrooms are found in Kay Cude Past, Al Past, and Sheila Bernal Guzmán, "A Bilingual Kindergarten Immersed in Print," *The Reading Teacher* 33 (1980), 907-13.

Chapter 5. How Computers Help Children Learn to Read, pp. 48-62.

1. Seymour Papert, *Mindstorms: Children, Computers, and Powerful Ideas* (New York: Basic Books, 1980).
2. R. Baird Shuman, "A Dozen Ways for English Teachers to Use Microcomputers," *English Journal* 74 (October 1985): 37-39.
3. George Mason, Jay S. Blanchard, and Danny B. Daniel, *Computer Applications in Reading*, 2d ed. (Newark, DE: International Reading Association, 1983). The first edition was published in 1979.
4. Leo Geoffrion and Olga Geoffrion, *Computers and Reading Instruction* (Reading, MA: Addison-Wesley, 1983).
5. Patricia N. Chrosniak and George W. McConkie, "Computer Assisted Reading with Reading Discouraged Children," Unpublished paper delivered at the annual meeting of the American Educational Research Association on April 1, 1985, in Chicago, Illinois, 7.
6. Frank H. Kasson, "The Typewriter: A Coming Necessity in Schools," *Education* 15 (June 1985): 615-22.
7. Dianne M. Kaake, "Teaching Elementary Age Children Touch Typing as an Aid to Language Arts Instruction," *The Reading Teacher* 36 (March 1983): 640-44.
8. J. L. Rowe, "Readin', Typin', and 'Rithmetic," *Business Education World* 39 (January 1959): 9-12.
9. Ted Kreiter, "Kiddies on the Keys," *The Saturday Evening Post* 253 (March 1981): 75, 103.
10. Dianne M. Kaake, "Teaching Elementary Age Children," 641. Kaake reports that her summer school typing courses ran for an hour a day, four days a week, for eleven weeks. However, in the normal classroom situation, especially with primary school students, smaller time increments are probably desirable.
11. Mark Grabe and Cindy Grabe, "The Microcomputer and the Language Experience Approach," *The Reading Teacher* 38 (February 1985): 509.
12. Curtis C. Dudley-Marling, "Microcomputers, Reading, and Writing: Alter-

natives to Drill and Practice," *The Reading Teacher* 38 (January 1985): 389.

13. Nancy J. Smith, "The Word Processing Approach to Language Experience," *The Reading Teacher* 38 (February 1985): 556.

14. Grabe and Grabe, "The Microcomputer," 510.

15. Lea M. McGee, "Awareness of Text Structure: Effects on Children's Recall of Expository Text," *Reading Research Quarterly* 17 (1982): 581ff. See also Priscilla A. Drum, Robert C. Calfee, and Linda K. Cook, "The Effects of Surfaced Structure Variables on Performance in Reading Comprehension Tests," *Reading Research Quarterly* 16 (1981): 486-514; and Jill Fitzgerald Whaley, "Readers' Expectations for Story Structure," *Reading Research Quarterly* 17 (1981): 90-114.

16. Grabe and Grabe, "The Microcomputer," 510.

17. Roger Farr, *Reading: Trends and Challenges*, 2d ed. (Washington, DC: National Education Association, 1986), 6-7.

18. *Ibid.*, 11.

19. *Ibid.*, 21.

20. Dudley-Marling, "Microcomputers," 388-89.

21. For an informative discussion of teaching spelling with microcomputers, see Roy A. Moxley and Pamela A. Barry, "Spelling with LEA on the Microcomputer," *The Reading Teacher* 38 (December 1985): 267-73.

22. Many useful spelling programs are also readily available. Among these are *Whole Brain Spelling* (Champaign, IL: Sublogic Communications); *Word Scramble* (Garden City, MI: T.H.E.S.I.S.); *Words for the Wise* (Genesco, NY: TYC Software); *Spelling Bee* (Agoura, CA: Edu-Ware Services); *Spelling Builder* (Greenwich, CT: Program Design); *Spelling Rules* (Dallas, TX: Micro Power and Light); *Rhymes and Riddles* (Cambridge, MA: Spinnaker Software); and *Instant Zoo* and *Magic Spells*, both available through Apple Computer dealers.

23. For a further discussion of this topic, see pp. 38-39.

24. George W. McConkie and David Zola, "Eye Movement Techniques in Studying Differences Among Developing Readers," in *Biobehavioral Measures of Dyslexia*, edited by D. Gray and J. Kavanagh (Parkton, MD: York Press, 1986); and N. Roderick Underwood and David Zola, "The Span of Letter Recognition in Good and Poor Readers," *Reading Research Quarterly* 21 (1986): 6-19.

25. See the section on paired reading in *Parental Involvement in Children's Reading*, edited by Keith Topping and Sheila Wolfendale (New York: Nichols, 1985), 109-159.

26. Judy Wedman, "Reading Software: What's Out There?" *Language Arts* 60 (April 1983): 516-17.

27. Ernest Balajthy, "Computer Simulations and Reading," *The Reading Teacher* 37 (March 1984): 590-93.

Chapter 6. The Language Experience Approach to Teaching Reading, pp. 63-74.

1. See particularly L. C. Ehri, "Word Consciousness in Readers and Prereaders," *Journal of Educational Psychology* 67 (1975): 204-12; and M. H. Holden and Walter H. McGinitie, "Children's Conceptions of Word Boundaries in Speech and Print," *Journal of Educational Psychology* 63 (1972): 551-57.

2. Roach Van Allen and Gladys C. Halvorsen, "The Language Experience Approach to Reading," Ginn and Company contributions to *Reading*, no. 27 (Lexington, MA: Ginn, 1961).

3. Jeanette Veatch, *Reading in the Elementary School*, 2d ed. (New York: John Wiley and Sons, 1978), 300. Veatch undoubtedly intended to say, "Children speak and *listen* before they write" rather than "Children speak and talk before they write."

4. Barbara Mallon and Roberta Berglund, "The Language Experience Approach to Reading: Recurring Questions and Their Answers," *The Reading Teacher* 37 (1984): 867-71.

5. Elaine Vilscek, "What Research Has Shown About the Language-Experience Program," in *A Decade of Innovative Approaches to Beginning Reading*, edited by Elaine Vilscek (Newark, DE: International Reading Association, 1968), 9-23.

6. Douglas E. Giles, "The Effects of Two Approaches to Reading Instruction upon the Oral Language Development of First Grade Pupils," *Dissertation Abstracts* 27 (1966): 139-A.

7. Harry T. Hahn, *Teaching Reading and Language Skills in Grades Two and Three* (East Lansing: Michigan State University, 1968), 1.

8. Gertrude Hildreth, "Linguistic Factors in Early Reading Instruction," *The Reading Teacher* 18 (1964): 172-78.

9. Veatch, *Reading in the Elementary School*, 385.

10. Wilma H. Miller, *Teaching Elementary Reading Today* (New York: Holt, Rinehart and Winston, 1984), 75.

11. Nicholas Anastasiow, *Oral Language: Expression of Thought* (Newark, DE: International Reading Association, 1971), 6.

12. Veatch, *Reading in the Elementary School*, 384.

13. As reported by Pat Cunningham, "Curriculum Trends in Reading," *Educational Leadership* 41 (April 1984): 83.

14. Carol Chomsky, "Write First, Read Later," *Childhood Education* 47 (1971): 296-99; Roy Moxley, *Writing and Reading in Early Childhood: A Functional Approach* (Englewood Cliffs, NJ: Educational Technology, 1982); and Pat Cunningham, "Writers Make Better Readers," a subheading in "Curriculum Trends in Reading," 92.

15. Miller, *Teaching Elementary Reading Today*, 66-67. See also Topping and

Wolfendale, *Parental Involvement in Children's Reading*.

16. Mark Grabe and Cindy Grabe, "The Microcomputer and the Language Experience Approach," *The Reading Teacher* 38 (February 1985): 509.

17. *Ibid.*, 510.

18. See Lea M. McGee, "Awareness of Text Structure: Effects on Children's Recall of Expository Text," *Reading Research Quarterly* 17 (1982): 581.

19. Curtis C. Dudley-Marling, "Microcomputers, Reading and Writing: Alternatives to Drill and Practice," *The Reading Teacher* 38 (1985): 389. See also Virginia Bradley, "Improving Students' Writing with Microcomputers," *Language Arts* 59 (1982): 732-43.

20. Roy A. Moxley and Pamela A. Barry, "Spelling with LEA on the Microcomputer," *The Reading Teacher* 38 (1985): 269.

21. Jane Hansen, "The Effects of Inference Training and Practice on Young Children's Reading Comprehension," *Reading Research Quarterly* 16 (1981): 391.

22. Eleanore S. Tyson and Lee Mountain, "A Riddle or Pun Makes Learning Words Fun," *The Reading Teacher* 36 (1983): 170.

23. *Ibid.*

24. Kay Cude Past, Al Past, and Sheila Bernal Guzmán, "A Bilingual Kindergarten Immersed in Print," *The Reading Teacher* 33 (1980): 907.

Chapter 7. Phonics and Reading Instruction, pp. 75-84.

1. Paul McKee, *Reading: A Program for the Elementary School* (Boston: Houghton Mifflin, 1966), 74. Some reading experts include more letters than these as regular. Dechant (see note 2 immediately below) includes *y* (as a consonant) and *z*. Edward Fry [*Elementary Reading Instruction* (New York: McGraw-Hill, 1977), 24] includes, along with *y* and *z*, *s* (as in *sit*), *c* (as in *cat*), and *g* (as in *get*). I omit *y* because it is generally a vowel, *z* because it represents two sounds (as in *zebra* and *azure*), *s* because it represents the /s/ sound (*sit*) and the /z/ sound (*its*), *c* because it represents the hard sound (*cat*) as well as the soft sound (*certain*), and *g* which can be hard (*gun*) or soft (*gem*).

2. Emerald Dechant, *Linguistics, Phonics and the Teaching of Reading* (Springfield, IL: Charles C. Thomas, 1969), 36.

3. *Ibid.* See also Richard D. Lambert and Barbara F. Freed, *The Loss of Language Skills* (New York: Newbury House, 1982), 76.

4. Albert J. Mazurkiewicz, *Teaching About Phonics* (New York: St. Martin's Press, 1976), 32.

5. See Gertrude Hildreth, *Teaching Reading* (New York: Holt, Rinehart and Winston, 1958). See also her "Some Misconceptions Concerning Phonics," *Elementary English* 36 (January 1957): 26-27.

6. Betty Berdiansky, Bruce Cronnell, and John Koehler, *Spelling-Sound Relations and Primary Form-Class Descriptions for Speech Comprehension Vocabularies of 6-9 Year Olds*, Technical Report No. 15 (Los Alamitos, CA: Southwest Regional Laboratory for Educational Research and Development, 1968).
7. For a fuller discussion of this matter, see Mazurkiewicz, *Teaching*, 31-32.
8. *Ibid.*, 69-71 and 32-33.
9. Jack Bagford, "The Role of Phonics in Teaching Reading," in *Reading and Realism*, edited by J. Allen Figurel (Newark, DE: International Reading Association, 1967), 83.
10. *Ibid.*, 85.
11. Franklin set forth his system in *Scheme for a New Alphabet and Reformed Mode of Spelling*, published in Philadelphia in 1768.
12. For a full discussion of spelling reform movements in the United States, see Dennis E. Baron, *Grammar and Good Taste: Reforming the American Language* (New Haven: Yale University Press, 1982), 68-98.
13. *A Century of Tribune Editorials* (Chicago: The Tribune Company, 1947), 64-65.
14. See "Thru's Through and So Is Tho," Editorial, *Chicago Tribune*, September 29, 1975, sec. 2, p. 2; and *A Century of Tribune Editorials*.
15. Sir James Pitman and John St. John, *Alphabets and Reading: The Initial Teaching Alphabet* (New York: Pitman, 1969), 117. The material quoted is reproduced in this book in the i. t. a. The writer has transcribed it into conventional English.
16. Edward Fry, *Elementary Reading Instruction*, 72.
17. Emery P. Bleismer and Betty H. Yarborough, "A Comparison of Ten Different Beginning Reading Programs in First Grade," *Phi Delta Kappan* 56 (1965): 500-504.
18. Jeanne Chall, *Learning to Read: The Great Debate* (New York: McGraw-Hill, 1967), 134. Chall refers to Chapter 3, "Research on Beginning to Read—Science or Ideology?"
19. *Ibid.*, 125.
20. Connie Juel and Diane Roper-Schneider, "The Growth of Letter-Sound Correspondence Knowledge in First Grade and Its Relation to Reading Achievement and Programs," in *New Inquiry in Reading Research and Instruction*, edited by Jerome A. Niles and Larry A. Harris (Rochester, NY: The National Reading Conference, 1982), 155.
21. *Ibid.*, 307.
22. William H. McGuffey, ed., *McGuffey's First Eclectic Reader*, rev. ed. (Cincinnati: Van Antwerp, Bragg, and Co., 1879), ii.
23. Mazurkiewicz, *Teaching*, 132.
24. Barbara Nemko, "Context Versus Isolation: Another Look at Beginning Readers," *Reading Research Quarterly* 19 (1984): 461-67.

Chapter 8. Linguistics and Reading Instruction, pp. 85-96.

1. Charles C. Fries, *Linguistics and Reading* (New York: Holt, Rinehart and Winston, 1963), 36.
2. Frank Smith, *Psycholinguistics and Reading* (New York: Holt, Rinehart and Winston, 1973), 1.
3. J. Richard Gentry, "Learning to Spell Developmentally," *The Reading Teacher* 34 (1981): 378-83.
4. Jean W. Gillet and Charles Temple, *Understanding Reading Problems: Assessment and Instruction* (Boston: Little, Brown, 1982), 170.
5. *Ibid.*, 178. See also Kristine F. Anderson, "The Development of Spelling Ability and Linguistic Strategies," *The Reading Teacher* 39 (1985): 142.
6. Clarence L. Barnhart, "The Story of the Bloomfield System," in *Let's Read: A Linguistic Approach*, edited by Leonard Bloomfield and Clarence L. Barnhart (Detroit: Wayne State University Press, 1961), 9.
7. Dolores Durkin, *Phonics, Linguistics, and Reading* (New York: Teachers College, Columbia University, 1972), 13.
8. The first example avoids the redundancy of the second in which *three* clearly indicates plurality and -*s* merely reiterates that plurality.
9. Charlton Laird, *The Miracle of Language* (New York: Premier Books, 1953), 159. Laird's italics.
10. Leonard Bloomfield, "Linguistics and Reading," *Elementary English Review* 19 (April 1942): 125.
11. Leonard Bloomfield, "Teaching Children to Read," in Bloomfield and Barnhart, *Let's Read*, 24. Bloomfield's italics.
12. J. N. Hook, "Spelling: Trial and Terror," in *The Teaching of High School English* (New York: Ronald Press, 1972), 417. See also Durkin, *Phonics*, 2.
13. Compare Bruno Bettelheim and Karen Zelan, *On Learning to Read: The Child's Fascination with Meaning* (New York: Alfred A. Knopf, 1982), 27; and Charles Elster and Herbert D. Simons, "How Important Are Illustrations in Children's Readers?" *The Reading Teacher* 39 (1985): 148.
14. Bloomfield and Barnhart, *Let's Read*, 32. Bloomfield's italics.
15. Ronald Wardhaugh, "Is the Linguistic Approach an Improvement in Reading Instruction?" in *Current Issues in Reading*, edited by Nila Banton Smith (Newark, DE: International Reading Association, 1969), 256.
16. Fries, *Linguistics*, 96. Fries's italics.
17. *Ibid.*, 94. Fries's italics.
18. *Ibid.*, 100. Fries's italics.
19. William S. Gray, *The Teaching of Reading: A Second Report*, 36th Yearbook of the National Society for the Study of Education, Part I (Bloomington, IL: Public School Publishing Co., 1937), 25-28.
20. Fries, *Linguistics*, 120. Fries's italics.
21. *Ibid.*, 121. Fries's italics.
22. *Ibid.*, 156.

23. Kenneth Goodman, "Miscue Analysis," in Smith, *Current Issues in Reading*, 269.

Chapter 9. Learning from Misreadings: A Look at Miscue Analysis, pp. 97-109.

1. Portions of this chapter appeared as Chapter 6, "Miscue Analysis as a Key to Understanding Reading Problems," in R. Baird Shuman, *Strategies in Teaching Reading: Secondary* (Washington, DC: National Education Association, 1978), 54-61. Copyright © 1978 by the National Education Association of the United States. Used with permission.
2. Noam Chomsky, *Syntactic Structures* (The Hague: Mouton, 1957).
3. Ronald Wardhaugh, "Is the Linguistic Approach an Improvement in Reading Instruction?" in *Current Issues in Reading*, edited by Nila Banton Smith (Newark, DE: International Reading Association, 1969), 263.
4. *Ibid.*
5. *Ibid.*, 264.
6. Kenneth Goodman, *The Psycholinguistic Nature of the Reading Process* (Detroit: Wayne State University Press, 1967).
7. Kenneth S. Goodman, "Analysis of Oral Reading Miscues: Applied Psycholinguistics," *Reading Research Quarterly* 5 (1969): 11.
8. *Ibid.*
9. *Ibid.*
10. *Ibid,* 19-26.
11. See Frank Smith, *Psycholinguistics and Reading* (New York: Holt, Rinehart and Winston, 1973), 80.
12. Goodman, "Analysis."
13. Carolyn L. Burke and Kenneth S. Goodman, "When a Child Reads: A Psycholinguistic Analysis," *Elementary English* 47 (1970): 121-29.
14. Rose-Marie Weber, "The Study of Oral Reading Errors: A Survey of the Literature," *Reading Research Quarterly* 4 (1968): 96-119.
15. Smith, *Psycholinguistics*, 80.
16. Kenneth S. Goodman, "A Linguistic Study of Cues and Miscues in Reading," *Elementary English* 42 (1965): 39-44.
17. Goodman, "Analysis," 16.
18. W. Nelson Francis, *The Structure of American English* (New York: Ronald Press, 1958), 556.
19. The decision in *Martin Luther King Junior Elementary School Children et al.* v. *Ann Arbor School District Board* found that Black students in the Ann Arbor Schools were being deprived of equal access to education because their teachers were not familiar with the dialect most of them spoke. The decision mandated that teachers in the district be taught Black English. The opinion is presented in full in Geneva Smitherman, ed., *Black English*

and the Education of Black Children and Youth: Proceedings of the National Invitational Symposium on the King Decision (Detroit: Harlow Press, 1981), 336-58.

20. Kenneth R. Johnson, "What Should Be Taught to Students Who Speak Black Dialect?" in *Questions English Teachers Ask*, edited by R. Baird Shuman (Rochelle Park, NJ: Hayden, 1977), 172.

21. *Ibid.*, 172-73.

22. William Labov, *The Study of Nonstandard English* (Champaign, IL: National Council of Teachers of English, 1970), 44. See also Marvin Cohn and Cynthia D'Alessandro, "When Is a Decoding Error Not a Decoding Error?" *The Reading Teacher* 32 (1978): 341-44.

23. Distributed by Vision Quest, Inc., 7715 North Sheridan Road, Chicago, IL 60626. For a fuller discussion of this matter, see R. Baird Shuman, ed., *Educational Drama for Today's Schools* (Metuchen, NJ: Scarecrow Press, 1978), 41-58.

24. Goodman, "Analysis," 14.

25. R. L. Allington, "Teacher Interruption Behaviors During Primary Grade Oral Reading," *Journal of Educational Psychology* 72 (1980): 371-77.

26. As reported by James V. Hoffman and Richard Clements, "Reading Miscues and Teacher Verbal Feedback," *The Elementary School Journal* 84 (1984): 421-37. The study is also reported on in James V. Hoffman and others, "Guided Oral Reading and Miscue Focused Verbal Feedback in Second-Grade Classrooms," *Reading Research Quarterly* 19 (1984): 367ff., and in James V. Hoffman, Sharon F. O'Neal, and Richard O. Clements, "The Effects of Differentiated Patterns of Verbal Feedback to Miscues on Word Identification Strategies and Success," in *New Inquiries in Reading Research and Instruction*, edited by Jerome A. Niles nd Larry A. Harris (Rochester, NY: The National Reading Conference, 1982), 145-51.

27. Hoffman and Clements, "Reading Miscues," 436.

28. James Peter Tortelli, "Simplified Psycholinguistic Diagnosis," *The Reading Teacher* 29 (1976): 637.

29. Laray Brown, "'Correctness' and Reading," *The Reading Teacher* 28 (1974): 277.

30. *Ibid.*, 278.

31. Aaron Lipton, "Miscalling While Reading Aloud: A Point of View," *The Reading Teacher* 25 (1972): 760. Lipton's italics.

32. For a more complete description of this useful technique, see Tortelli, "Diagnosis," 637-39.

33. Kenneth S. Goodman, ed., *Miscue Analysis: Applications to Reading Instruction* (Urbana, IL: National Council of Teachers of English, ERIC Clearinghouse on Reading and Communication Skills, 1973). [ED 080 973]

34. Gerard M. Ryan, "An Experimental Investigation of the Psycholinguistic Model of the Reading Process," in *Perspectives on Reading: A Symposium on the Theory and Teaching of Reading*, edited by Desmond Swan (Dub-

lin: The Glendale Press, 1982), 86.

35. Yetta Goodman, "Using Children's Reading Miscues for New Teaching Strategies," *The Reading Teacher* 23 (1970): 455.

Chapter 10. Dialects and Early Reading Instruction, pp. 110-23.

1. Dell Hymes, ed., *Pidginization and Creolization of Languages* (Cambridge: Cambridge University Press, 1971).
2. *Martin Luther King Junior Elementary School Children et al.* v. *Ann Arbor School District Board* (463 F. Supp. 1027 [1978] and 473 F. Supp. 1371 [1979]), as reproduced in Geneva Smitherman, ed., *Black English and the Education of Black Children and Youth: Proceedings of the National Invitational Symposium on the King Decision* (Detroit: Harlow Press, 1981), 336-57. The material quoted is from pp. 337-38.
3. *Ibid.*, 343.
4. See particularly Geneva Smitherman, *Talkin' and Testifyin': The Language of Black America* (Boston: Houghton Mifflin, 1977); J. L. Dillard, *Black English: Its History and Use in the United States* (New York: Random House, 1972); and William Labov, *Language in the Inner City* (Philadelphia: University of Pennsylvania Press, 1972). Also of exceptional importance and historical significance are James Sledd, "Bi-Dialectism: The Linguistics of White Supremacy," *English Journal* 59 (1969): 1309-29; Roger Shuy and Ralph W. Fasold, *Language Attitudes: Current Trends and Prospects* (Washington, DC: Georgetown University Press, 1973); Ralph Fasold, *Tense Marking in Black English* (Washington, DC: Center for Applied Linguistics, 1972); and Raven McDavid and Virginia McDavid, "The Relationship of the Speech of American Negroes to the Speech of Whites," *American Speech* 26 (February 1951): 3-17.
5. See William Labov, "Academic Ignorance and Black Intelligence," *Atlantic Monthly* 229 (June 1972): 65.
6. For additional information, see Roger W. Shuy, "A Linguistic Background for Developing Beginning Reading Materials for Black Children," in *Teaching Black Children to Read*, edited by Joan Baratz and Roger W. Shuy (Washington, DC: Center for Applied Linguistics, 1969), 128-29; Dillard, *Black English*, 281; and Kenneth R. Johnson, "What Should Be Taught to Students Who Speak Black Dialect?" in *Questions English Teachers Ask*, edited by R. Baird Shuman (Rochelle Park, NJ: Hayden, 1977), 172.
7. Judy Iris Schwartz, "An Investigation of Attitudes on the Use of Black Dialect," *Research in the Teaching of English* 9 (1975): 201.
8. J. Steptoe, *Stevie* (New York: Harper and Row, 1969).
9. Education Study Center, *Friends, Old Tales,* and *Ollie* (Washington, DC: The Center, 1970).
10. Schwartz, "An Investigation."

11. *Ibid.*, 207.
12. *Ibid.*, 206-207.
13. *Ibid.*, 201.
14. Dorothy S. Strickland and William A. Stewart, "The Use of Dialect Readers: A Dialogue," in *Black Dialects and Reading*, edited by Bernice W. Cullinan (Urbana, IL: ERIC Clearinghouse on Reading and Communication Skills, 1974), 147.
15. *Ibid.*, 150.
16. *Ibid.*, 147.
17. *Ibid.*
18. Jane W. Torrey, "Illiteracy in the Ghetto," *Harvard Educational Review* 40 (1970): 254. Italics added.
19. *Ibid.*, 253, 256. Italics added.
20. Jane W. Torrey, "Black Children's Knowledge of Standard English," *American Educational Research Journal* 20 (1983): 627-43.
21. Herbert D. Simons and Kenneth R. Johnson, "Black English Syntax and Reading Interference," *Research in the Teaching of English* 8 (1974): 353.
22. Martin Deutsch, "The Disadvantaged Child and the Learning Process," in *Education in Depressed Areas*, edited by A. H. Passow (New York: Teachers College Press, Columbia University, 1963), 163-80.
23. S. Engelmann, "How to Construct Effective Language Programs for the Poverty Child," in *Language and Poverty: Perspectives on a Theme*, edited by F. Williams (Chicago: Markham, 1970), 102-22.
24. Christopher Clausen, "Schoolmarms, the Linguists, and the Language," *Midwest Quarterly* 19 (1978): 233.
25. Beatrice K. Levy, "Is the Oral Language of Inner City Children Adequate for Beginning Reading Instruction?" *Research in the Teaching of English* 7 (1973): 52.
26. See Roy C. O'Donnell, William J. Griffin, and Raymond G. Norris, *Syntax of Kindergarten and Elementary School Children: A Transformational Analysis* (Champaign, IL: National Council of Teachers of English, 1967), 44-45.
27. Levy, "Oral Language," 56-57.
28. O'Donnell, Griffin, and Norris, *Syntax*, 45.
29. Levy, "Oral Language," 55-56.
30. *Ibid.*, 59.
31. For a full discussion of how teacher attitudes affect learning outcomes, see Robert Rosenthal and Lenore Jacobson, *Pygmalion in the Classroom: Teacher Expectation and Pupils' Intellectual Development* (New York: Holt, Rinehart & Winston, 1968).
32. Laray Brown, "'Correctness' and Reading," *The Reading Teacher* 28 (1974): 278.
33. Simons and Johnson, "Black English Syntax," 357. See also James V. Hoff-

man and Richard Clements, "Reading Miscues and Teacher Verbal Feedback," *The Elementary School Journal* 84 (1984): 437-38.

34. Annabel A. Bixby, "Do Teachers Make A Difference?" *Childhood Education* 54 (1978): 288. Italics added.

35. Philip C. Schlechty and Helen E. Atwood, "The Student-Teacher Relationship," *Theory Into Practice* 16 (1977): 286.

36. Labov, "Academic Ignorance," 66. Italics added.

37. Torrey, "Illiteracy," 258.

38. Barbara J. Shade, "Social-Psychological Traits of Achieving Black Children," *Negro Educational Review* 29 (April 1978): 80.

39. See particularly Labov, *Language in the Inner City* and William Labov, *The Study of Nonstandard English* (Champaign IL: National Council of Teachers of English, 1970).

40. Shade, "Social-Psychological Traits," 82. Italics added.

41. It is interesting to consider this contention in light of L. Dummett, "The Enigma—The Persistent Failure of Black Children in Learning to Read," *Reading World* 24 (October 1984): 31-37.

42. Shade, "Social-Psychological Traits," 85.

43. *Ibid.*

44. Nicholas J. Anastasiow and Michael L. Hanes, *Language Patterns of Poverty Children* (Springfield, IL: Charles C. Thomas, 1976), 145. Italics added.

45. James S. Coleman, *Equality of Educational Opportunity* (Washington, DC: Department of Health, Education and Welfare, 1966). Also see Coleman's *Power and Structure of Society* (New York: Norton, 1963).

46. This list is from R. Baird Shuman, *Strategies in Teaching Reading: Secondary* (Washington, DC: National Education Association, 1978), 53. Copyright © 1978 by the National Education Association of the United States. Used with permission.

Chapter 11. The Pros and Cons of Basal Readers, pp. 124-35.

1. Nila Banton Smith, *Reading Instruction for Today's Children* (Englewood Cliffs, NJ: Prentice-Hall, 1963), 99.

2. James D. Hart, *The Popular Book: A History of America's Literary Taste* (New York: Oxford University Press, 1950), 153.

3. Wilma H. Miller, *Teaching Elementary Reading Today* (New York: Holt, Rinehart & Winston, 1984), 87.

4. *Ibid.*

5. Patricia M. Russavage, Larry L. Lorton, and Rhodessa L. Millham, "Making Responsible Instructional Decisions About Reading: What Teachers Think and Do About Basals," *The Reading Teacher* 39 (1985): 315.

6. Maryann Murphy Manning and Gary L. Manning, *Reading Instruction in the Middle School: A Whole School Approach* (Washington, DC: National